ST GREGORY OF NAZIANZUS

Poems on Scripture

ST VLADIMIR'S SEMINARY PRESS
Popular Patristics Series
Number 46

The Popular Patristics Series published by St Vladimir's Seminary Press provides readable and accurate translations of a wide range of early Christian literature to a wide audience—students of Christian history to lay Christians reading for spiritual benefit. Recognized scholars in their fields provide short but comprehensive and clear introductions to the material. The texts include classics of Christian literature, thematic volumes, collections of homilies, letters on spiritual counsel, and poetical works from a variety of geographical contexts and historical backgrounds. The mission of the series is to mine the riches of the early Church and to make these treasures available to all.

Series Editor
BOGDAN BUCUR

Associate Editor
IGNATIUS GREEN

* * *

Series Editor
1999–2020
JOHN BEHR

ST GREGORY OF NAZIANZUS

Poems on Scripture

GREEK ORIGINAL AND
ENGLISH TRANSLATION

Translation and Introduction by
BRIAN DUNKLE, S.J.

ST VLADIMIR'S SEMINARY PRESS
YONKERS, NEW YORK
2012

Library of Congress Cataloging-in-Publication Data

Gregory, of Nazianzus, Saint.
    [Poems. English & Greek. Selections]
    St. Gregory of Nazianzus, poems on scripture / translation and introduction by
Brian Dunkle.
        p. cm. — (Popular patristics series, ISSN 1555–5755 ; no. 46)
        "Greek original and English translation."
        ISBN 978–0–88141–433–2
        1. Gregory, of Nazianzus, Saint—Translations into English. 2. Christian
poetry, Greek—Translations into English. 3. Theology—Poetry. I. Dunkle,
Brian. II. Title. III. Title: Poems on scripture.

    PA3998.G73A23 2012
    881'.01—dc23

                                                                2012032243

COPYRIGHT © 2012 BY

ST VLADIMIR'S SEMINARY PRESS
575 Scarsdale Road, Yonkers, NY 10707
1-800-204-2665
www.svspress.com

ISBN 978–088141–433–2
ISSN 1555–5755

PRINTED IN THE UNITED STATES OF AMERICA

For
My Parents

Acknowledgements

This project began as a thesis submitted for the degree of Licentiate of Sacred Theology at the Boston College School of Theology and Ministry. Many thanks to my advisor, Khaled Anatolios, and my reader, Fr Brian Daley, S.J., for their corrections, comments, and encouragement; to Blake Leyerle and Albertus Horsting, who helped me as the initial project expanded; to Fr Joseph T. Lienhard, S.J., whose course in the Cappadocian Fathers some years ago occasioned my first encounter with the Theologian's verse; and to Fr John Behr and Fr Benedict Churchill at St Vladimir's Seminary Press for supervising the publication. Last I thank John and Margaret Dunkle, loving parents and careful proofreaders.

Contents

Introduction   9

The Poems   34

Other Biblical Poems   76

Select Bibliography   158

Introduction

Gregory of Nazianzus (*c.* 326–389), preacher, poet, bishop, and saint, was born and spent much of his life on the country estate of Karbala, near the center of the Roman province of Cappadocia, in modern-day Turkey.[1] Renowned as the "Theologian"—a title he shares with John the Evangelist in the Orthodox Church—Gregory has had a profound and lasting influence on the history of Christian doctrine and spirituality.[2] His preaching, a model of rhetorical skill and theological subtlety, treats themes central to the articulation of pro-Nicene orthodoxy in the late fourth century; in particular, his Five Theological Orations, which he delivered while Bishop of Constantinople, clarified Christian thought on the divinity of the Holy Spirit and the relations within the Triune Godhead. His letters, which detail the political and ecclesiastical background to the theological disputes of his time, have likewise drawn steady interest from scholars looking to understand the era's social dynamics.

[1] John McGuckin, *St. Gregory of Nazianzus: An Intellectual Biography* (Crestwood, NY: St. Vladimir's Press, 2001), is the definitive English biography; also valuable are Paul Gallay, *La vie de Saint Grégoire de Nazianze* (Paris: E. Vitte, 1943); Jean Bernardi, *Saint Grégoire de Nazianze: le Théologien et son temps, 330–390.* Initiations aux Pères de l'Eglise (Paris: Editions du Cerf, 1995); Francesco Trisoglio, *Gregorio di Nazianzo il Teologo*, Studia patristica Mediolanensia 20 (Milan: Vita e pensiero, 1996); with special attention to Gregory's poetry, see Francis Gautier, *La Retraite et le Sacerdoce chez Grégoire de Nazianze* (Turnhout: Brepols, 2002). The year of his birth is disputed; see Brian Daley, S.J., *Gregory of Nazianzus*, The Early Church Fathers (London: Routledge, 2006), 190 n.5, who also offers an excellent and concise introduction to the Theologian's life.

[2] For John Damascene, to speak "theologically" was to cite Gregory's writings; e.g. *On the Divine Images,* Treatise 1.8.

His poems, by contrast, are less widely known, although they have recently become the subject of closer study.[3] More than 17,000 lines of Gregory's verse survive, including poems that summarize and explain his theology, as well as verse epistles, laments, numerous epitaphs, and personal reflections, which are some of the earliest examples of autobiography.[4]

Gregory's poetic corpus also includes the few instances where Gregory explicitly presents a reading of the biblical narrative. These seventeen scriptural poems, numbered I.1.12 to I.1.28 in Migne's *Patrologia Graeca*, form the heart of the translation that follows.[5] They have otherwise been scarcely noted in the scholarship, except to be dismissed as "tedious" and "mnemonic verse."[6] To my knowledge, no English translation of the set exists in publication.[7] After a brief

[3] Including a number of doctoral dissertations: Christos Simelidis (DPhil, Oxford, published as a monograph) *Selected Poems of Gregory of Nazianzus: I.2.17; II.1.10, 19, 32: A Critical Edition with Introduction and Commentary* (Göttingen: Vandenhoeck & Ruprecht, 2009); Susan Abrams Rebillard, "Speaking for Salvation: Gregory of Nazianzus as Poet and Priest in his Autobiographical Poems" (PhD Diss. Brown University, 2003); Preston Edwards "Ἐπισταμένοις ἀγορεύσω: On the Christian Alexandrianism of Gregory of Nazianzus" (PhD Diss. Brown University, 2003) also treats some of the poems; J. Prudhomme, "L'oeuvre poétique de Grégoire de Nazianze: héritage et renouveau littéraires" (PhD Diss. Université Lumière Lyon, 2006).

[4] Indeed, very few examples of Greek Christian poetry and hymnody antedate Gregory; for a list, see Simelidis, *Selected Poems*, 29.

[5] In 1842 the Maurist Dom Caillau organized Gregory's poems in vol. 37 and vol. 38 of the PG in two books: I. The *theologica*, comprising the *dogmatica* and the *moralia* and II. The *historica*, comprising the *poemata de seipso* (the poems "on himself") and the *poemata quae spectant ad alios* (those that "look to others"). In addition, he included the epigrams and the *Christus patiens*, a drama in cento form whose authenticity is disputed; see H. Werhahn "Dubia und Spuria bei Gregor von Nazianz," *Studia Patristica 7* (Berlin, 1966), 337–347. Caillau's ordering only very loosely corresponds to any presentation found in the manuscript tradition; for a recent discussion, see Guillaume Bady, "Ordre et desordre des *poemes* de Gregoire le Théologien," in Incontro di studiosi dell'antichità cristiana, *Motivi e forme della poesia cristiana antica tra scrittura e tradizione classica: XXXVI Incontro Di Studiosi dell'antichità cristiana, Roma, 3–5 Maggio 2007* (Studia ephemeridis "Augustinianum" 108; Rome: Institutum patristicum Augustinianum, 2008), 337–348.

[6] Donald Sykes, *St. Gregory of Nazianzus: Poemata Arcana, Introduction, translation and commentary* ed. by Claudio Moreschini (Oxford: Clarendon, 1997), 58.

[7] There is an Italian translation by Claudio Moreschini, *Gregorio Nazianzeno: Poesie*, vol.1 (Rome: Città nuova, 1994), 47–65.

overview of Gregory's family background and formation in pagan
and Christian culture, I introduce the poems, focusing on their major
themes, their catechetical motives, and their literary and theological
merit. In addition to the translating these poems, I also include a num-
ber of Gregory's poems that reveal his attitude toward Scripture and
his techniques for applying the biblical text to his own situation.

Gregory's family and background

Some familiarity with Gregory's family background is needed before
examining his theological project, both because Gregory frequently
wrote about his upbringing, including paeans to his parents and
siblings, and because family affairs otherwise dominated much of
his career.[8] Gregory was born into a thoroughly Christian house-
hold.[9] His mother Nonna descended from a noble Christian lineage
and distinguished herself by her piety and good works. His father,
Gregory the Elder, converted to Christianity from the sect of the
Hypsistarians, that is, those devoted to the *hypsistos*, the "Most
High One," before Gregory's birth, and later became a prominent
politician and bishop.[100] Through their influence, Gregory, his sister
Gorgonia, and his younger brother Caesarius received a Christian
formation from childhood.[11]

Gregory's father was instrumental in most of the major decisions
of his life, including his ordination as a priest and then as a bishop

[8] Gregory includes autobiographical details in many of his writings; two poems in
particular are lengthy presentations of his personal history: II.1.1 "On his own affairs,"
and II.1.11 "On his own life."

[9] On the cultural background, see McGuckin, *Gregory of Nazianzus*, 1–84;
Gautier, *Le Retraite et le Sacerdoce*, 257–267.

[10] Gregory gives an account of his father's religious background in his funeral
oration (*Or.* 18), delivered in 374.

[11] Gregory presents his childhood formation in certain poems and letters;
scholars today use the material only with caution; see Abrams Rebillard, "Speaking
for Salvation," 1–15 and Neil McLynn, "A Self-Made Holy Man: the Case of Gregory
Nazianzen," *JECS* 6 (1997): 463–483. On Gregory's childhood education, Bernhard
Wyß, "Gregor von Nazianz," *RAC* vol.12, 797–798.

(of Sasima in Asia Minor, a seat in which he was never formally installed), and his appointment to the see of Constantinople in 380.[12] Although Gregory seems to have clashed with his father on certain theological and political decisions, including his own ordination, he expresses a warm fondness for his parents, even dedicating thirty-six epitaphs to his mother.[13] Indeed, his frequent attempts to break family ties in order to embrace monastic life never took him very far; he secluded himself in a region rather close to his family estate, where he was easily, perhaps intentionally, located by Church officials.[14]

Moreover, familiarity with Gregory's background helps one understand the particularly personal nature of his theological project. Because of the many autobiographical references in his writings, Gregory's work is frequently the subject of psychological readings, which find him a sensitive, even self-obsessive, case.[15] Much of his thought has a degree of introspection that goes beyond the standard self-reflection characteristic of his age, presenting him, in the words of Bernardi, as "une âme tourmentée."[16] Especially in his poems, Gregory scrutinizes his struggles and accomplishments in light of his relationship to Christ and the Church. While recent scholarship has questioned the sincerity and accuracy of Gregory's self-presentation, most agree that Gregory distinguishes himself from his contemporaries by the degree of his insistence on the symbolic meaning of his struggles and accomplishments.[17] At the same time, he often offers his life as a model for his readers to imitate.

---

[12]McGuckin offers an extensive and psychologizing treatment of Gregory's relationship with his father in his biography; *St. Gregory of Nazianzus*, 1–34.

[13]Among them is a passage from the autobiographical *c.* II.1.11, 68–92.

[14]See Brooks Otis, "The Throne and the Mountain," *Classical Journal* 56 (1961): 146–165.

[15]See Abrams Rebillard's evaluation of such approaches, "Speaking for Salvation," 1–15.

[16]Bernardi, *Grégoire*, 314; the author also wonders whether Gregory was "le premier des romantiques," 326.

[17]Most recently, see Bradley K. Storin, "In a Silent Way: Asceticism and Literature in the Rehabilitation of Gregory of Nazianzus," *JECS* 19 (2011): 225–257.

Gregory's education

By all accounts, Gregory received a thorough classical formation, first during his childhood near Nazianzus and then during his stays at Palestinian Caesarea, Alexandria, and, most extensively, Athens.[18] While in Greece Gregory studied letters with leading figures in the Roman Empire, perhaps among them Julian, who would become the famous "Apostate" emperor in 361. Prominent grammar teachers, known as sophists, prepared their students in the *enkyklios paideia*, the comprehensive formation that comprised grammar, dialectic, rhetoric, geometry, arithmetic, astronomy, and, often, music.[19] Various studies have revealed the extent of Gregory's knowledge of classical literature.[20] He was intimately familiar with Homer and the ancient poets, including Pindar, Aeschylus, and Sophocles. He also knew the classical orators, especially Demosthenes, enough to imitate and adapt their language and rhetorical periods in his own speeches.

At Athens Gregory's passion for composing literature also matured. In the autobiographical poem "On his own life" (II.1.11), he records his initial infatuation with writing:

> While my cheek was still beardless, a passionate love
> of letters
> possessed me. Indeed I sought to make bastard letters
> serve as assistants to the genuine ones.[21]

[18]For a succinct account of his formation see Wyß, "Gregor von Nazianz," 794–798.

[19]Wyß, "Gregor von Nazianz," 797.

[20]Wyß, "Gregor von Nazianz"; Kristoffel Demoen, *Pagan and Biblical Exempla in Gregory Nazianzen: A Study in Rhetoric and Hermeneutics,* Corpus Christianorum 2 (Turnhout: Brepols, 1996).

[21]II.1.11, 112–114, trans. Carolinne White, *Gregory of Nazianzus, Autobiographical Poems*, Cambridge medieval classics 6 (Cambridge: Cambridge University Press, 1996), 19.

Words, both written and spoken, became Gregory's main preoc-
cupation. More importantly, the quest to employ classical learning
in order to articulate Christian thought would occupy the rest of his
career.[22] In his letters, poems, and speeches, Gregory sought to put
his classical training at the service of Christian revelation.

During his studies, Gregory not only mastered the content of
classical learning, but he also acquired classical ways of reading.
Gregory learned to engage literature by interpreting it through
close attention to the language of the author within the unity of his
corpus. A well-trained student deciphered any problematic word,
phrase, or passage by locating parallels in the text. Once the student
could establish what the author meant in a broader context, he
would be better equipped to resolve the ambiguity in the puzzling
portion. Gregory's fastidious attention to words emerges from this
early training.

Gregory's particular reception of Hellenistic, especially Alexan-
drian, philological techniques has been the subject of recent study.[23]
While earlier scholarship conjectured that Gregory most likely knew
classical literature indirectly, through anthologies, recent studies
show his first-hand familiarity with, among others, Callimachus,
Apollonius, and Theocritus.[24] Gregory's poems are full of words
and phrases culled from these authors, which he often reconfig-
ures in inventive and suggestive ways. Gregory not only refers to
important classical and Hellenistic writers, but he also retrieves and
adapts their method of allusion and reference. In this way Gregory
resembled many of his late antique contemporaries, who prized a
finely wrought system that reworked this Hellenistic heritage.[25]

[22]For more on Gregory's pursuit of the reconciliation, see Gautier, *Le Retraite et
le Sacerdoce*, 169–175 and 268–280.

[23]So Edwards, "Christian Alexandrianism," 30–45; Simelidis, *Selected Poems*,
30–46; Gennaro d'Ippolito, "Gregorio di Nazianzo: la poesia come tetrafarmaco," in
Incontro Augustinianum, Motivi e forme, 393.

[24]Simelidis, *Selected Poems*, 31, calls Gregory's engagement with Callimachus an
"obsession"; for an inventory of references to these authors, see Demoen, *Pagan and
Biblical Exempla*.

[25]Indeed, it is this culture of reference that led, in part, to Gregory's unpopularity

Even as he appropriated the classical Greek tradition into his writings, Gregory the Christian drew from the Bible as the ultimate source for his rhetoric. He was among the first generation to be formed in a Christian culture that was beginning to supplant the dominant pagan worldview. As Frances Young has documented, despite real ambivalence toward classical authors, Christians did not simply reject Greek *paideia*, but rather transformed it in order to promote learning based on the Bible.[26] Christian readers applied the same techniques to reading Scripture that they had employed when reading Homer or Demosthenes; the Bible was seen as a unity, which could furnish the attentive reader with all the tools necessary for its own interpretation. Thus, even as he was alluding to Callimachus, Gregory could communicate Christian content in his writings.

It is surprising, then, that despite his thorough engagement with the Bible Gregory has left us virtually no extended scriptural exegesis or commentary.[27] Moreover, scholars, both ancient and modern, agree that Gregory made profound contributions to the history of biblical interpretation; Jerome, the Father of Western biblical exegesis, names Gregory "my master in the Sacred Scripture," while Brian Daley, in a recent study on Gregory's use of Scripture, affirms that the Theologian is "a quintessentially Biblical thinker and writer."[28]

in the nineteenth and early twentieth century, when an educated audience generally prized originality; see Edwards, "Christian Alexandrianism," 5–13.

[26] *Biblical Exegesis and the Formation of Christian Culture*, 49–118; see also her "*Paideia* and the Myth of Static Dogma," in Sarah Coakley and David Palin, eds. *The Making and Remaking of Christian Doctrine: Essays in Honour of Maurice Wiles* (Oxford: Clarendon, 1993), 265–283.

[27] The only extended treatment of a biblical passage appears in *Or.* 37 on Mt 19.1–12, which is, in fact, more a reflection on Christian marriage than on Scripture itself; see Frederick Norris, "Gregory Nazianzen: Constructing and Constructed by Scripture," in *The Bible in Greek Christian Antiquity*, edited by Paul Blowers (Notre Dame, Ind.: NDU Press, 1997), 149; Norris notes that the twelfth-century Elias of Crete attributes to Gregory a treatise called *The History of Ezechiel the Prophet*, which does not survive.

[28] Jerome, *In Isaiam* 3; see Paul Gallay, "La Bible dans l'oeuvre de Grégoire de Nazianze le Théologien," in *Le monde grec ancien et la Bible*, edited by Claude Mondésert (Paris: Beauchesne, 1984), 316; Daley, "Walking through the Word of God: Gregory of Nazianzus as a Biblical Interpreter," in *The Word Leaps the Gap*, ed. by

Yet few have attempted to examine Gregory's use of the Bible in real depth.[29]

Such a study must engage Gregory's poems on Scripture. Although these verses lack any sustained, penetrating exegesis, they do reveal some of Gregory's basic assumptions in his approach to the sacred text. For their part, these attitudes are informed by Gregory's broader account of his reasons for composing verse in order to do theology. Thus, some background on Gregory the poet will help us understand the motives and techniques that guide his particular contribution to early Christian biblical theology.

Gregory's poetry and fourth-century Christian culture

Gregory explains his decision to compose verse in his poem II.1.39, "On Matters of Measure."[30] After describing how his enemies often mock his versifying, Gregory claims that writing poetry brings him four distinct benefits: first, it allows him some relief from the pressures of daily life; second, it shows the pagans that Christians can compose verse as accomplished as the ancient classics; third, poetry makes complicated theology more accessible and attractive to young audiences; fourth, it offers Gregory a certain consolation in his old age.[31] To be sure, this list is not exhaustive and may be intentionally selective: scholars have detected a rather transparent apologetic

J. Ross Wagner, A. Katherine Grieb, and C. Kavin Rowe (Grand Rapids: Eerdmans, 2008), 530.

[29]The most extensive treatment is Demoen, *Pagan and Biblical Exempla*; also Gallay: "La Bible dans l'oeuvre de Grégoire de Nazianze," 313–334; Norris "Constructing and Constructed by Scripture," 149–162.

[30]McGuckin, "Gregory: The Rhetorician as Poet," 195 suggests this title for poem II.1.39, which the PG editors, following the manuscripts, label *Εἰς τὰ ἔμμετρα* (PG 37.1330–1338). The poem is thoroughly treated in the scholarship; see Cecilia Milovanovic-Barham, "Gregory of Nazianzus: *Ars Poetica (In suos versus, carm.* 2.1.39)," *JECS* 5 (1997): 497–510, for bibliography and introduction.

[31]McGuckin, "Gregory: The Rhetorician as Poet," 210 includes a fifth reason, based on lines 58–59: an invitation to the wise to enter Gregory's mind.

motive for Gregory's verse and for this "programmatic" poem in particular.[32] Still, the third motive deserves special attention: Gregory uses verse in order to render abstract theology available and appealing to a broad, uneducated audience.

Here Gregory seems inspired by at least two models. The first is a standard trope in classical pedagogy. Pagan authors often defended didactic verse as a way to "sugar-coat" unpleasant ideas with entertaining and attractive literary ornament. Lucretius, for instance, defends his *De Rerum Natura*, a first-century BC exposition of Epicureanism, by appealing to the practice of sweetening medicine for a sick child: just as the child will not accept the pill unless it has been dipped in honey, so the unlettered audience will not embrace a philosophy that seems "bitter" unless it has first been sweetened by pleasant language and verse.[33] The poetic form, then, offered clear rhetorical advantages in the transmission of Christian doctrine.

Second, Gregory's poetic project resides in a wider Christian cultural program that emphasized the catechetical end of all literature. By the second half of the fourth century, Christian authors show a pressing concern to compile and communicate a coherent body of teaching both to their children, who were to be raised in a Christian milieu, and to catechumens, who were encountering the faith for the first time.[34] The great mystagogies mark one attempt to create this corpus for large groups of initiates into the Christian faith, when eminent preachers such as Ambrose of Milan and Theodore of Mopsuestia introduced catechumens to the mysteries of the liturgy.[35]

[32]See, e.g., Federico Fatti, "Il cane e il poeta: Gregorio Nazianzeno e Massimo il Cinico (su Greg. Naz. carm. II, 1, 39 e II, 1, 41)," in Incontro Augustinianum, *Motivi e forme*, 310–317.

[33]*De Rerum Natura*, 1.933–950; some form of the trope dates at least to Plato, *Laws*, 2.659e.

[34]For an overview, see Antonio Quacquarelli, *Reazione pagana e trasformazione della cultura (fine IV secolo. d.C.)* (Bari: Edipuglia, 1986), esp. 125–142.

[35]For an introduction, see Edward Yarnold, *The Awe-Inspiring Rites of Initiation: The Origins of the RCIA*, 2nd ed. (Collegeville, MN: Liturgical Press, 1994), 1–54.

Theologians were thus offering more systematic and unified accounts of Christian doctrine, including simple versions and summaries, often in verse, of the Church consensus on Christ's divinity and belief in the Trinity. Such summaries were necessary not only for mass dissemination, but also to respond to rival teachings promoted by heretics. Ephrem the Syrian, for instance, saw his liturgical hymns as an orthodox alternative to the heretical doctrines of Bardaisan, the Marcionites, the Manicheans, and his contemporaries, the Arians.[36] Gregory, then, was composing his verse just as the Church was generating a coherent body of *paideia* that was intended to supplement, if not replace, classical Greek learning and to render orthodox teaching in accessible form, in response to rival threats.[37]

Some of these efforts, including Gregory's didactic poems, may have also had a more proximate inspiration. In 362 Emperor Julian ("the Apostate") issued his famous "School Law," which forbade Christian educators to teach the pagan classics. According to contemporary sources, Julian passed the edict with the claim that Christians could not honestly teach pagan learning if they did not believe that it was true; since they rejected the pagan divinities, they would fail to communicate the central "faith" of pagan literature.[38] In theory, at least, the law threatened Christians who were intent on political advancement and who were living in a culture where fluency in the classics was still essential social capital.[39]

---

[36]Indeed, the heretic Bardaisan, in order to promote his own doctrines, composed hymns, which appear to have been popular among those living in Mesopotamia and help account for the rapid spread of his peculiar brand of Christianity in the region during the third and fourth century.

[37]Franz Xaver Portmann, *Die göttliche paidagogia bei Gregor von Nazianz* (St. Ottilien: Eos verlag der Erzabtei, 1954), 17–33, presents Gregory's broader pedagogical project, especially as found in *Or.* 2; on Gregory creating a body of Christian *paideia*, see McGuckin, "Gregory: The Rhetorician as Poet," 200–201.

[38]Julian's law is recorded in *Cod. Theod.* 13.3.5; cf. Ammianus Marcellinus, *Res Gestae*, 22.10.

[39]See Henri Marrou, *A History of Education in Antiquity* (Madison, WI: University of Wisconsin Press, 1982), 309–11.

While the legislation was soon overturned after Julian's early death in 363, the move seems to have aroused a Christian response that persisted for decades.[40] The fifth-century historians Sozomen and Socrates report that Christian authors began to compose literature that rivaled classical texts in technique and artistry, while eliminating the pagan philosophy and mythology that those texts communicated.[41] The most famous attempt came from a father and son, both named Apollinaris.[42] The two, it seems, translated the entire Bible into the standard classical literary genres.[43] Thus, they paraphrased the Old Testament according to the model of Homer and the tragedians, and made the New Testament into a Platonic dialogue.[44] While the final product does not survive—perhaps because its authors were later linked to a Christological heresy—their effort provides an intriguing parallel with Gregory's theological and scriptural poetry.[45]

Other authors before Gregory had attempted biblical verse and paraphrases. The Latin author Juvencus had already composed a gospel paraphrase early in the fourth century, but most biblical Christian verse appears after Julian's School Law was overturned. For instance, the Latin cento of Proba, composed around 370,

[40]See Demoen, *Pagan and Biblical Exempla*, 23 on Gregory's response to Julian in *Or.* 4

[41]Sozomen, *Historia Ecclesiastica*, 5.18; Socrates, *Historia Ecclesiastica*, 3.16.

[42]It was the younger of the two who would later gain notoriety for the eponymous heresy that denied the existence of a human soul in the Incarnate Christ.

[43]On the background, see Gianfranco Agosti, "L'epica biblica nella tarda antichità greca: autori e lettori nel IV e V secolo," in *La Scrittura infinita: Bibbia e poesia in età medievale e umanistica*, ed. Francesco Stella (Firenze: SISMEL, Edizioni del Galluzzo, 2001), 67–101; P. Sneck, "A More Charitable Verdict: Review of N. G. Wilson, *Scholars of Byzantium*," in idem, *Understanding Byzantium* (London: Ashgate, 2003), 163–178, argues that the account of the Apollinaris project is legendary.

[44]Socrates *Historia ecclesiastica* 3.16.1–5.

[45]Their paraphrases do not even seem to have survived into the fifth-century; later historians claim to have no first-hand experience of their verse. Yet John Zonaras in the twelfth century linked the Gregorian and Apollinarian efforts together; *Epitome Historion* (61.13–62.4); see Simelidis, *Selected Poems*, 26–27, who maintains that Gregory's attempt comes in response to Apollinaris' effort, as is stated by Gregory's 6th/7th-century biographer, Gregory the Presbyter.

reworked phrases from Virgil's *Aeneid* to compose a Christian poem on the transcendence of God.[46] Paulinus of Nola may have likewise intended his psalm paraphrases to respond to the threat and the indirect insult posed by Julian's edict.[47] Christians began to recognize that a common, aesthetically accomplished body of literature could communicate their faith to future generations while remaining unspoiled by pagan influence.

The poems on Scripture

Gregory's poems on Scripture should be seen as part of this broader cultural project. To introduce neophytes and children to Christian culture, Church educators needed to present the basics of the scriptural narrative. Thus, while Gregory has left us very few examples of sophisticated exegesis and commentary—the kind of sophisticated engagement with Scripture that generally attracts scholarly attention—his scriptural poems show that he was concerned with the first steps in this pedagogical program.[48]

Scholars have long dismissed these poems not only because they seem elementary and easy, but also because Gregory's scriptural verse, often little more than biblical paraphrase for quick memorization, can be dull. As Sykes puts it, they "show how tedious mnemonic verse can be."[49] Indeed, the metrical Latin translation of Gregory in the *Patrologia Graeca* ends abruptly while Gregory is merely ren-

[46]For a recent study, see David Meconi, S.J., "The Christian Cento and the Evangelization of Classical Culture," *Logos* 7:4 (2004): 109–131; Agosti, "L'epica biblica," 74–77.

[47]See Roger Green, *Latin epics of the New Testament: Juvencus, Sedulius, Arator* (Oxford: Oxford University Press, 2006), 143–148.

[48]The poems are among those numbered I.1.20–27, with I.1.12, "On the Genuine Books of Scripture," perhaps serving as a preface PG 37; a rare study of this group is Roberto Palla, "Ordinamento e polimetria delle poesie bibliche di Gregorio Nazianzeno," *Wiener Studien* 102 (1989): 169–185. Donald Sykes has published a series of articles on the didactic elements in Gregory's poems; for a sample, see "Gregory Nazianzen as Didactic Poet," *Studia Patristica* 16.2 (1985): 433–437.

[49]Sykes, *Poemata Arcana*, 58.

dering the Matthaean and Lucan genealogies—name by name—in verse form; Billius, the sixteenth-century translator, decides to stop, "Because anyone can look for [these names] in the Gospels, and because they consist entirely of Hebrew names, from which you can hardly say how far the Latin Muses recoil."[50] The bland and monotonous verse utterly fails to match Gregory's rhetorical skill in his greatest orations and letters.

Yet they deserve closer attention. While the final version may seem disappointing, the process of composition must have been rigorous and demanding. This rigor is precisely one of the reasons that Gregory gives for writing verse in the first place, as he notes in his programmatic poem "On Matters of Measure": choosing his words carefully helps him control his language in general.[51] These scriptural poems, like much of his verse, are models of verbal asceticism.[52]

A *"helpful plaything for children"*

Moreover, Gregory's precision and control aim at a simplicity that fosters memorization and understanding.[53] Lengthy gospel pericopes are rendered in one or two lines of hexameter or elegiacs so that they might be retained more easily as discrete moments in a catalogue.[54] Gregory often repeats vocabulary, including simple words and phrases such as μέγας and Χριστός ἄναξ, poetic *formulae* that would help a student commit the verse to memory. He will place similar phrases in the same metrical position, which then become easy for the student to organize in parallel with identical patterns.

[50]*Nobis eamdem, carminibus exprimere minime placuit, tum qui cuivis ab evangelistis petere licet, tum quia tota Hebraicis nominibus constat, a quibus vix dici potest, quantum Latinae musae abhorreant* [my translation]; *PG* 37.485, n.60.

[51]C. II.1.39, 35–37.

[52]Gautier, *La Retraite et le Sacerdoce*, 172–189.

[53]Basil (*Greater Rule* 15.2) and Jerome (ep. 107.4) both encourage committing the miracles and genealogies to memory; see Palla, "Ordinamento e polimetria," 175.

[54]On "concision" as the main feature of Gregory's poetry, see Trisoglio, *Gregorio il Teologo*, 185.

There is some hint that Gregory's meter itself is more easily memorized. Gregory's hexameters are especially dactylic, that is, each foot is very often resolved into dactyls, rather than left as long spondees.[55] Homer's verse, for instance, usually pairs two dactyls with every spondee, while in Gregory the ratio is more like 5 to 1.[56] In the poems on Scripture, the ratio is even higher, around six resolved dactyls for every spondee.[57] Gregory's preference for resolved dactyls in these poems appears at least to help students recite or even sing the verses.

Gregory is not simply content to make his didactic verse easily accessible and committed to memory. Following the established method of didactic verse, these poems incorporate certain ornaments to make them more pleasant. In this way, Gregory sprinkles his verse with delicate linguistic markers that encourage some familiarity with classical learning, so central to Gregory's own formation. He introduces his audience not only to the outlines of Scripture, but also to certain arcane elements of classical literature. Although they may not suit every grown-up's taste, his poems are, as he puts it, "a helpful plaything for children."[58]

The pedagogical order of the poems on Scripture

Further evidence for this pedagogical end appears in the probable original order of these poems. Borrowing from a suggestion of Roberto Palla, I present them in my translation organized as a sequence that would help a student memorize the central scriptural

[55]Simelidis, *Selected Poems*, 56, gives some statistics on the patterns and frequencies of dactyls in the corpus.

[56]Sykes, *Poemata Arcana*, 62.

[57]To be sure, the recitation of ancient quantitative verse cannot be immediately conflated with modern experience of poetry, with its stress accents that tend to have an effect of impression through repetition. See Milovanovic-Barham, "Gregory of Nazianzus: *Ars Poetica*," 497–510.

[58]As the acrostic ἐσθλὸν ἄθυρμα νέοις present in poem I.2.31, 31–47; also II.1.39, 39, where Gregory calls poetry a τερπνὸν . . . φάρμακον ("a pleasant medicine").

narrative. This order, I propose, would teach the student that exegesis should end in a personal engagement with the word of God as the source of salvation. Moreover, this strategy appears elsewhere in Gregory's poetry, revealing something of Gregory's approach to Scripture in general: God's self-revelation must not remain propositional, historical, and remote, but must be appropriated personally by each believer.[59]

The carefully chosen language of these poems would prepare students not only to remember the outlines of Scripture but also to introduce them to vocabulary and constructions that would help them grasp classical learning, namely, the Hellenistic *paideia* in which Gregory himself was formed.[60] Employing Homeric and Callimachean words, even when metrically equivalent, biblical alternatives were available, Gregory prepares his students to engage the pagan classics, but from a Christian point of view. Indeed, in literature, especially in late antiquity, where a single word could signal a myriad of allusions, Gregory introduces his audience to the very strategies of textual reference.

"The Parables of Christ According to All the Evangelists" (I.1.27)

The final poem in the gospel series departs from the previous seven. Here Gregory no longer paraphrases Scripture, but rather presents a personal encounter with the Gospel parables. Writing in the first person, Gregory rereads twenty-nine of the parables that he has just presented in the previous scriptural verses.[61] By concluding the collection with this "final prayer," as Palla calls it, Gregory offers a clue

[59]This parallels his well-known autobiographical style and tendency to apply scriptural morals to himself, especially in his biblical interpretation; see Daley, "Walking through the Word," 519–520; for a somewhat skeptical view of that persona, see McLynn, "A Self-Made Holy Man," 463–483.

[60]On Gregory's language in general, see Simelidis, *Selected Poems*, 47–54.

[61]With a section reprised in another poem ("Exhortation to virgins," I.2.2); see Demoen, *Biblical and Pagan Exempla*, 188, who argues that the reprised portion is original to I.1.27.

to his approach to Scripture in general:[62] he teaches his audience that Scripture must be personally appropriated to be learned at all.

In I.1.27, Gregory offers a series of petitions, praises, and laments that relate himself immediately to the Gospel parables. He opens the poem by using the language of parables to ask God for support: he worries that his foundation might be placed on sand (Mt 7.24–27); he could be the seed sown among the thorns or under the direct heat of the sun (Mt 13.3–6). He then praises the mustard seed for the marvelous symbolism it contains (Mt 13.31–32). He adds another petition for help, to be fished from the sea of troubles, and not to be thrown overboard with the useless catch (Mt 13.47–50). He includes some exegesis, such as his own clarification of the parable of the two sons who were asked to work in the vineyard (Mt 21.28–32): the one who works in the garden after saying he would not is obviously greater than the one who says he would and does not do so. "But," Gregory adds, "greater in my eyes, and more pleasing than both to the father is the one who receives the command, and carries out the wish" (ll. 36–41).[63] He places himself at the heart of the wedding feast (Mt 22.1–14), repeating the phrase, "May I take part in this!"[64] He adds for his readers: "As well as whoever is my friend!"[65] Gregory's passion for God's word draws him to the heart of the Scripture, where he invites the audience to join him. The parables recorded by the evangelists are not mere accounts of Christ's teaching on earth. They are "about" Gregory and those who read Scripture as Gregory does.[66]

Moreover, the very structure of the poem introduces the reader to the project of personalizing Scripture. There is a regular, reliable

[62]Palla, "Ordinamento e polimetria," 184.

[63]Κρείσσων μὲν ἐμοὶ, γλυκίων δὲ τοκῆϊ Ἀμφοτέρων, ὃς ἔδεκτο, καὶ ἐξετέλεσσεν ἐέλδωρ (ll.40–42; PG 37.501).

[64]τοῦδ' ἀντιάσαιμι ἔγωγε (l.44; PG 37.501).

[65]καὶ ὃς φίλος ἐστὶν ἔμοιγε! (1.45; PG 37.502).

[66]For a comprehensive study of this sort of reading, see Andrew Hofer, OP, "Herald of the Word: Gregory of Nazianzus Evoking Christ" (PhD Dissertation, University of Notre Dame, 2010).

pattern: the first half of each unit summarizes the argument of the parable, including any salient details and vocabulary; the second half applies the moral to the author of the poem and, by implication, to the reader. For instance, Gregory presents the parable of the fishermen and the catch:

> I know as well the world that falls within the net,
> which, on command from Christ the king, while sailing,
> the fishers of men surround by casting out the net,
> so as to drag them from ocean depths, and then to bid
>   those
> swimming on the bitter waves of this life to come to Christ.
> But when you judge the catch, dividing it in half
> may you not cast me far away, as though I were a useless
>   fish,
> but place me safe in baskets, guarded by the king. (24–31)

Gregory shifts from presenting an allegorical reading of the passage to the moral interpretation. His student, arriving at poem I.1.27 after the series of poems on Scripture, would be prepared to receive this method of reading Scripture as he received the content of the Gospels. Not only would the student learn a catalogue of stories, but he would also absorb a way of reading them.

The pedagogy of this concluding poem corresponds to the exhortation that probably served as a preface to the collection, Gregory's poem on the genuine books on Scripture. Gregory opens the poem by reminding his audience to devote their lives to Scripture:

> Let your mind and your tongue always dwell among
> the divine words. For God has given this prize for your
>   struggles,
> a little light to see even some hidden thing, or what is best,
> to be spurred on by the pure God's great commands,

> or third, by these concerns you draw your heart from
>   earthly things.[67]

God's words are not abstract laws or norms of conduct, but rather they "spur on" Gregory and the Christian who reads them rightly.

Personal reading of Scripture in other poems

This practice appears throughout Gregory's poetic corpus, whenever he encourages a robust and personal appropriation of Scripture.[68] Examples abound, some more sophisticated than others. Often Gregory merely applies biblical exempla to himself. In his poem, "On the Silence during Lent" (II.1.34), for instance, Gregory refers to the sons of Aaron and Uzzah, who were punished for impurity in offering sacrifice; Gregory prays, "I tremble dreadfully at these things and fear that I will suffer/ for not being pure when touching upon the pure Trinity" (ll. 103–104).[69] Here Gregory takes the Old Testament exemplum as a warning against allowing the impure to approach anything holy, thereby extending the rules for ritual purity to the object of theology itself, that is, the divine Trinity. Moreover, the object of the warning is not "priests" in general, but Gregory in particular. As an example of such a "personal reading," I include an extended poem, "Against Anger," in which Gregory invokes numerous scriptural exempla in the quest to mollify or eradicate his tendency to wrath.

In other cases, Gregory actually identifies with a personality in Scripture, making himself the object of the narrative. Writing on the soul, Gregory refers to the Word's creation of the human being in

[67]I.1.14, l.1–4.

[68]Daley, "Walking through the Word of God," 519–520; see Young, *Biblical Exegesis*, 248 who discusses the "characteristic of the Antiochene" to expect that every tale had a moral ordered to the improvement of the reader; also Ackermann, *Die didaktische poesie*, 66–82.

[69]Trans. White, *Autobiographical Poems*, 173.

Genesis 2, yet applies the story to the creation of his own soul: "Then he took up a portion of new-formed earth/ and with immortal hands set up my shape,/ to which he then imparted his own life."[70] God not only created Adam in Genesis; He made Gregory, and, by extension, the reader reciting the poem and identifying with the first person. In concluding his poem on the Two Covenants (I.1.9), he refers the theological reason for the double covenant to his own condition: if he were capable of fulfilling the Old Law, he would have had no need for the New:

> But now, since God did not make me a god,
> but fashioned me inclinable both ways, and slanted,
> he therefore supports me, along with many others,
> who possess one grace of the baptism given to mortals.[71]

The New Law is more than an abstract instruction; God sent the Church and sacraments to help sinners, and to help Gregory above all.[72]

Recognizing the presence of this exegetical strategy elsewhere in Gregory's verse helps us better understand his poetry as a whole. The pervasive interiority of the poems can occasionally suggest a certain self-absorption and narcissism. As Gregory himself puts it in *Oration* 26: "I have a habit of relating everything to my own situation."[73] Scholars have argued convincingly that Gregory deployed this strat-

---

[70]I.1.8, ll. 70–72; Ὡς ἄρ' ἔφη, καὶ μοῖραν ἑλὼν νεοπηγέος αἴης, Χείρεσιν ἀθανάτῃσιν ἐμὴν ἐστήσατο μορφὴν, Τῇ δ' ἄρ' ἑῆς ζωῆς μοιρήσατο; trans. Gilbert, *On God and Man*, 65.

[71]I.1.9, ll. 85–88; Νῦν δ', οὐ γάρ με θεὸν τεῦξεν Θεὸς, ἀλλά μ' ἔπηξεν Ἀμφιρεπῆ, κλιτόν τε, τὸ καὶ πλεόνεσσιν ἐρείδει, Ὧν ἓν καὶ λοετροῖο βροτοῖς χάρις; trans. Gilbert, *On God and Man*, 74.

[72]This approach, I believe, informs the orations as well, where series of biblical exempla are readily organized to apply to Gregory's particular audience. It would be helpful to examine the effect that the shift from the first-person emphasis of the poems to the second person in the orations and letters has on Gregory's technique. All this is beyond the present essay.

[73]Cited by Demoen, *Pagan and Biblical Exempla*, 289.

egy in his autobiographical verse to impress potential allies with his personal sanctity and thereby to defend his theological positions against his rivals' attacks; by emphasizing his spiritual and saintly credentials, Gregory indirectly justifies the doctrine he champions.[74] Gregory makes a point of presenting his own life in terms of the life of Christ in the Gospels: like Jesus, Gregory suffers persecution; like Jesus, Gregory sails on a turbulent sea; like Jesus, he goes into the desert; the list of parallels is extensive. Gregory may well contrive to present himself as a holy man, that is, an unimpeachable authority in matters of the faith and, indeed, in matters of politics as well.

Yet we should not assume that Gregory is somehow in bad faith when he speaks of his own life in terms of the life of Christ. The personal appropriation of Scripture in his poems (and, likewise, in his orations and letters) is not necessarily some disingenuous construction aimed to shore up his personal power. The presence of this strategy in the scriptural verse, aimed at educating children, shows the extent of his commitment to this sort of exegesis. Close study of the structure of corpus presented here suggests that Gregory believed everyone, from the youngest child to his learned audiences to Gregory himself, the advanced Christian, should read the Gospels in this personal way. The culmination of individual study of the life, death, and resurrection of Christ must be the personal embrace of that life.

Psalms and Laments

Gregory's personal reading is especially evident in many of the *threnoi*, or laments, that appear in the poems "on himself" (the *Poemata de seipso* in the PG). Critics have often treated the long complaints of these poems as evidence of Gregory's melancholic and even narcissistic personality. While there may be some merit to reading these poems as personal records, we should also recognize

[74]E.g. Abrams Rebillard, "Speaking for Salvation," 79–129.

their generic biblical traits, especially their resemblance to the many laments that appear in the psalter. When Gregory calls on God to forgive his many sins, to heal his many illnesses, and to bring punishment on his enemies, he is adopting the voice of the supplicant in distress. We must, therefore, be especially wary of culling these verses for details about the Theologian's personal life. To be sure, Gregory occasionally includes references to specific sufferings he must endure.[75] Yet the end of these poems is much more accurately located in his desire to apply the biblical voice to his own narrative. In my translation I have included a number of these laments.

For similar considerations I have included some of Gregory's hymns of praise. Like the laments, these poems witness Gregory's attempts to sing to the blessed Trinity according to the model of the psalter. Indeed, I would be inclined to group Gregory's "dogmatic" poems among these hymns, since they seem primarily intended to extol the greatness of the divine Persons rather than to expound their attributes in a systematic fashion. These poems, however, have attracted much more attention in the literature and are readily available in an excellent English translation.[76]

Conclusion

Close study of these biblical poems shows Gregory at his most deliberate and elementary. As such, they witness to what Gregory viewed as most essential to his broader cultural project. These are the ABCs of his theology, or, at least, of his approach to teaching Scripture. At the same time, they are, to some extent, the ABCs of his poetry as well. When viewed among Gregory's theological pursuits, the poems on Scripture are not simply occasional or frivolous entertainments. Linguistic and metrical markers show that they

[75]Cf. II.1.27 (PG 37.128), which refers to his exile from the church of Anastasia in Constantinople.

[76]Sykes, *Poemata Arcana*.

were meant to be accessible and easily put to memory, with some light stylistic touches enlivening the project for young learners. Yet a more serious hermeneutical claim undergirds Gregory's efforts: meditation on the Scriptures applies the teachings of revelation to the individual's condition. Amidst the debates over Gregory's preference for Alexandrian allegory or Antiochene "plain" reading,[77] close attention to these poems reveals that, irrespective of his exegetical preference, Gregory the Theologian was trained to turn the words of Scripture on himself, and looked to share his training with new students of the Bible.

Of course, one may dismiss didactic verse out of hand as somehow substandard, vulgarizing propaganda. Yet Gregory's poems were remarkably effective, both pedagogically and aesthetically. For the Byzantines their value in the classroom was never questioned. Since their composition, these poems have been recognized as a ready source for instructive and edifying material, and employed to teach Christian students. Not only were they transmitted continuously among the Byzantines and appeared frequently in the schools, they were extremely popular among the Renaissance humanists, edited and translated even more thoroughly than the pagan classics.[78] Indeed, Aldus, the first editor of the poems, esteems them for their capacity for educating young people in Christian virtue and theological discourse, "useful for living blessedly and well."[79]

At a time when theological literacy and familiarity with Scripture is at a notable low, we might do well to retrieve some of Gregory's zeal for composing a program of Christian formation that transmits the essentials of the faith while incorporating elements of our Western cultural heritage, just as Gregory incorporated Homer and Callimachus into his scriptural poems. We might look to fashion a method

---

[77] For some background to this debate, see Demoen, *The Bible and Greek Classics*, 237–267.

[78] The first edition of Gregory's poems was from Aldus Manutius in 1504; see Edwards, "Christian Alexandrianism," 24–27.

[79] Edwards, "Christian Alexandrianism," 25.

of communicating the truths of the faith that is somehow "a sweet plaything," yet that does not compromise theological rigor.[80]

Alternatively, Gregory's approach shows the importance of a holistic approach to Scripture. In an age when biblical scholarship tends to fragment the sacred text into sources and forms, we do well to follow the Theologian's model. Reading the Bible as a broad and coherent narrative, we come closer to the attitude that the ancients maintained, the Bible as a unified book.[81]

Text

Producing the critical edition of Gregory's poems has proven a very slow and cumbersome project, first begun in Poland in 1905.[82] Since 1981, a group of scholars at the University of Münster under the direction of Dr. Martin Sicherl have been laboring to produce the stemmata of the various Groups of the poems in preparation for publishing a comprehensive edition. While some of their conclusions have been published, much work remains. By a certain irony, especially given the lack of attention to Gregory's poems in the past century, much of the difficulty in producing the critical edition arises from Gregory's unparalleled popularity in the Byzantine era: so many manuscripts exist and appear to have mutually influenced subsequent copies that it is difficult to establish priority in order to generate an accurate and comprehensive stemma of the poems' manuscripts.[83]

[80]The Internet provides one venue for such a project; various "rhyming Bible" projects have emerged. See, for instance, http://www.kyleholt.com/the-bible-in-rhyme.

[81]Robert Louis Wilken, *The Spirit of Early Christian Thought* (New Haven: Yale University Press, 2005), 61–66.

[82]For the story of the Krakow Edition, see Edwards, "Christian Alexandrianism," 13–16.

[83]For a summary of the history of research on the editions, including the relevance of Syriac translations, see Simelidis, *Select Poems*, 88–99; for the stemma for Group I, see Höllger, *Die handschriftliche überlieferung*, vol. 2, 180.

For this reason, I must rely on Migne's text from the *Patrologia Graeca*, based on the edition of the Maurists under the direction of Dom Caillau, which is printed on pages facing my English translation. In a few instances I have printed readings in the text, while acknowledging the original reading in a footnote. Still, the essential element of this project is the translation.

Except for I.1.12, "On the genuine books of Scripture" and I.1.35, "Invocation before the reading of Scripture" none of the poems from the *carmina theologica* in this volume has, to my knowledge, a published English translation. The poems from the *carmina moralia* have been translated recently by Susan Abrams Rebillard in a still-unpublished dissertation;[84] I draw on some of her suggestions in my version. The PG also prints two Latin translations below the Greek. The first is a line-by-line literal rendering of the original, made by the Maurist editors. I occasionally rely on their suggestions where the Greek is ambiguous or inscrutable. The second version is a verse translation from Billius (Jacques de Billy), an aristocrat, humanist, and monk (1535–1581), who translated Gregory within the broader cultural project of the Counter-Reformation.[85] This version is both learned and loose, and therefore less useful to me as I attempt a literal and accurate rendition. For poem I.2.25, "Against Anger," I rely on the careful notes of Michael Oberhaus.[86]

In most of the poems, I have attempted to be as faithful to the Greek as possible.[87] This of course results in an English version that is not especially poetic and even, at times, stilted. Still, I decided that close attention to the specifics of Gregory's vocabulary would be more helpful for scholars interested in his influences and theological intentions. At the same time, I have kept the meter loosely iambic to communicate something of the flow of the verses that Gregory

[84]"Speaking for Salvation."

[85]On Billius, see Edwards, "Christian Alexandrianism," 33–43.

[86]*Gegen den Zorn*, 39–194.

[87]I follow some of the recommendations for translating Gregory offered by Nonna Verna Harrison, "Book Reviews: On Translating Gregory of Nazianzus," *St Vladimir's Theological Quarterly* 51 (2007): 123–131.

suggests by his rather "bouncy" hexameters. I am rather free in translating certain particles and conjunctions. In particular, I will ignore καί for my own metrical reasons when Gregory seems to use the conjunction *metri causa*. It would be beyond the scope of this work to match Gregory's literary competence in English verse.

Ποιήματα

I.1.35. Ἐπίκλησις πρὸ τῆς τῶν Γραφῶν ἀναγνώσεως.
(*dubium* PG 37.517–518)

Κλῦθι, Πάτερ Χριστοῦ πανεπίσκοπε, τῶνδε λιτάων
Ἡμετέρων· μολπὴν δὲ χαρίζεο σῷ θεράποντι
Θεσπεσίην. Ζαθέην γὰρ ἐς ἀτραπὸν ἴχνος ἐλαύνων
Οὗτος, ὃς αὐτογένεθλον ἐνὶ ζωοῖς θεὸν ἔγνω,
5 Καὶ Χριστὸν θνητοῖσιν ἀλεξίκακον βασιλῆα·
Ὅς ποτ᾽ ἐποικτείρας μερόπων γένος αἰνὰ παθόντων
Πατρὸς ὑπ᾽ ἐννεσίῃσιν ἑκὼν ἠλλάξατο μορφήν.
Γίγνετο δὲ θνητὸς Θεὸς ἄφθιτος, εἰς ὅ κε πάντας
Ταρταρέων μογέοντας ὑφ᾽ αἵματι λύσατο δεσμῶν.
10 Δεῦρ᾽ ἴθι νῦν, ἱερῆς καὶ ἀκηρασίης ἀπὸ βίβλου
Ψυχὴν σὴν ἀτίταλλε θεοπνεύστοις ἐνὶ μύθοις.   [518]
Ἔνθα γὰρ ἀθρήσειας ἀληθείης θεράποντας
Ζωὴν ἀγγελέοντας ὑπ᾽ οὐρανομήκεϊ φωνῇ.

The Poems

I.1.35. Invocation before the reading of Scripture
(PG 37.517–518)

Attend, O all-seeing Father of Christ, to these our petitions.
Be gracious to your servant's evening song;
for I am one who sets his footstep on the sacred
paths, who knows God to be the only self-generate among the
     living
5   and Christ to be the king who wards off ills from mortals.
He who once, with mercy on the dread race of suffering
     mortals,
willingly altered his form upon the Father's offer.
Incorruptible God, he became a mortal, in order that by his
     blood
he might free all who toil from the chains of Tartarus.
10   Come now and tend to your servant's soul
with inspired accounts from the book of holiness and purity.
For thus you might gaze on your servants of the truth
proclaiming true life with a voice as high as heaven.

I.1.12. Περὶ τῶν γνησίων βιβλίων τῆς θεοπνεύστου Γραφῆς.
(PG 37.472–474)

Θείοις ἐν λογίοισιν ἀεὶ γλώσσῃ τε νόῳ τε
Στρωφᾶσθ'· ἢ γὰρ ἔδωκε Θεὸς καμάτων τόδ' ἄεθλον,
Καί τι κρυπτὸν ἰδεῖν ὀλίγον φάος, ἢ τόδ' ἄριστον,
Νύττεσθαι καθαροῖο Θεοῦ μεγάλῃσιν ἐφετμαῖς·
5   Ἢ τρίτατον, χθονίων ἀπάγειν φρένα ταῖσδε μερίμναις.
Ὄφρα δὲ μὴ ξείνῃσι νόον κλέπτοιο βίβλοισι
(Πολλαὶ γὰρ τελέθουσι παρέγγραπτοι κακότητες),
Δέχνυσο τοῦτον ἐμεῖο τὸν ἔγκριτον, ὦ φίλ', ἀριθμόν.
Ἱστορικαὶ μὲν ἔασι βίβλοι δυοκαίδεκα πᾶσαι
10   Τῆς ἀρχαιοτέρης Ἑβραϊκῆς σοφίης.
Πρωτίστη, Γένεσις, εἶτ' Ἔξοδος, Λευιτικόν τε.   [473]
Ἔπειτ' Ἀριθμοί. Εἶτα Δεύτερος Νόμος.
Ἔπειτ' Ἰησοῦς, καὶ Κριταί. Ῥοὺθ ὀγδόη.
Ἡ δ' ἐνάτη δεκάτη τε βίβλοι, Πράξεις βασιλήων,
15   Καὶ Παραλειπόμεναι. Ἔσχατον Ἔσδραν ἔχεις.
Αἱ δὲ στιχηραὶ πέντε, ὧν πρῶτός γ' Ἰώβ·
Ἔπειτα Δαυΐδ· εἶτα τρεῖς Σολομωντίαι·
Ἐκκλησιαστής, Ἄισμα καὶ Παροιμίαι.
Καὶ πένθ' ὁμοίως Πνεύματος προφητικοῦ.
20   Μίαν μέν εἰσιν ἐς γραφὴν οἱ δώδεκα·
Ὡσηὲ κ' Ἀμὼς, καὶ Μιχαίας ὁ τρίτος·
Ἔπειτ' Ἰωὴλ, εἶτ' Ἰωνᾶς, Ἀβδίας,
Ναούμ τε, Ἀββακούμ τε, καὶ Σοφονίας,

I.1.12. On the genuine books of divinely inspired Scripture
(PG 37.472–474)[1]

O let your mind and tongue dwell among divine
phrases. For God has given this reward for the effort,
just a little light to see something hidden, or, what's best,
to be spurred on by the pure God's awesome commands,
5   or third, that by these concerns you may draw your heart from
        earthly things.
And that your mind might not be stolen by strange books
(for many are full of interpolated evils)
receive, my friend, this list of mine of the approved number.
For there are together twelve books of history
10   that treat the more ancient Hebrew wisdom.
The first is Genesis, then Exodus, then Leviticus,
then Numbers, then Deuteronomy,
then Joshua, Judges, and Ruth is eighth,
the ninth and tenth books are the acts of the Kings.[2]
15   And Chronicles. Then last you have Ezra.[3]
And then five books of verse of which the first is Job;
then the book of David; then the three books of Solomon:
Ecclesiastes, the Canticle, and Proverbs.
Likewise there are five books of the prophetic spirit,
20   twelve together are in a single text:
Hosea, Amos, and Micah is third,
then Joel, then Jonah, then Obadiah,
then Nahum, then Habakkuk, then Zephaniah,

---

[1]Gilbert, *On God and Man*, 85–86, offers his own version. In the manuscript organization of Gregory's corpus, this poem appears at the beginning of Group III, which I discuss in the introduction, and Group XVIII. The poem appears in other manuscripts under Gregory's name, but often lacks the first five introductory lines.

[2]Today these two books of the "acts of Kings" are divided into 1 and 2 Samuel and 1 and 2 Kings.

[3]Ezra or Esdras is variously divided in subsequent canonical lists into Ezra, Nehemiah, and 1 and 2 Esdras.

Ἁγγαῖος, εἶτα Ζαχαρίας, Μαλαχίας.
25 Μία μὲν οἴδε. Δευτέρα δ᾽ Ἡσαΐας.
     Ἔπειθ᾽ ὁ κληθεὶς Ἱερεμίας ἐκ βρέφους.   [474]
     Εἶτ᾽ Ἰεζεκιὴλ, καὶ Δανιήλου χάρις.
     Ἀρχαίας μὲν ἔθηκα δύω καὶ εἴκοσι βίβλους,
     Τοῖς τῶν Ἑβραίων γράμμασιν ἀντιθέτους.
30 Ἤδη δ᾽ ἀρίθμει καὶ νέου μυστηρίου.
     Ματθαῖος μὲν ἔγραψεν Ἑβραίοις θαύματα Χριστοῦ·
     Μάρκος δ᾽ Ἰταλίῃ, Λουκᾶς Ἀχαϊάδι·
     Πᾶσι δ᾽ Ἰωάννης, κήρυξ μέγας, οὐρανοφοίτης.
     Ἔπειτα Πράξεις τῶν σοφῶν ἀποστόλων.
35 Δέκα δὲ Παύλου τέσσαρές τ᾽ ἐπιστολαί.
     Ἑπτὰ δὲ καθολικαὶ, ὧν, Ἰακώβου μία,
     Δύω δὲ Πέτρου, τρεῖς δ᾽ Ἰωάννου πάλιν·
     Ἰούδα δ᾽ ἐστὶν ἑβδόμη. Πάσας ἔχεις.
     Εἴ τι δὲ τούτων ἐκτὸς, οὐκ ἐν γνησίαις.

I.1.14. Μάστιγες Αἰγύπτου. (PG 37.475–476)

     Μάστιγας Αἰγύπτοιο κακόφρονος αἰὲν ἀρίθμει,
     Ὡς κεν ὑποτρομέῃς κάρτεϊ τῷ μεγάλῳ.
     Αἵματι μὲν πρώτιστον ὕδωρ ἐρυθαίνετο γαίης,
     Δεύτερον αὖ βατράχους ἔβρασεν οὐλομένους.
5   Τὸ τρίτον αὖ, σκνίπεσσιν ἀὴρ καὶ γαῖα καλύφθη.
     Καὶ κυνόμυια φάνη τέτρατον ἐξαπίνης.   [476]
     Πέμπτον, τετραπόδεσσιν ἐπέχραε λυγρὸς ὄλεθρος.
     Φλυκτίδες ἀνθρώπων σώμασιν, ἕκτον ἄχος.

then Haggai, then Zachariah, then Malachi,
25   these are all one. The second is Isaiah.
Jeremiah, then, called from the womb,
then Ezekiel, and then the grace of Daniel.
I have set down twenty-two Old books,
equal in number to the Hebrews' alphabet.
30   Come then and number [the books] of the new mystery,
Matthew wrote the marvels of Jesus for the Jews.
Mark for Italy, Luke for Greece,
John, the great herald, heaven-haunting, wrote for all.[4]
Next the Acts of the wise Apostles,
35   and then the letters, fourteen of Paul,
then seven catholic, with one from James,
two from Peter, three from John again;
Jude's is seventh. You have them all.
If it's anything else, then it's not genuine.

I.1.14. The plagues of Egypt (PG 37.475–476)

Always number the plagues of evil-hearted Egypt,
so that you might tremble before God's great might.
First the water of the land reddened with blood (Ex 7.14–25).
Second [Egypt] spewed forth ruinous frogs (Ex 7.25–8.11).
5   Then, third, the earth and the sky were hidden by gnats
      (Ex 8.12–15),
and fourth the dog-fly suddenly appeared (Ex 8.20–32).
Fifth, a murderous plague struck four-legged creatures
      (Ex 9.1–7).
Boils on the bodies of men are the sixth distress (Ex 9.8–12).

[4]John's epithet, οὐρανοφοίτης ("dwelling in Heaven"), which refers to the mystical quality of the gospel, may also suggest a connection to the Evangelist's authorship of the Apocalypse, where he reports his heavenly vision; this book is otherwise not mentioned in this list. See Frank Thielmann, "The Place of the Apocalypse in the Canon of St. Gregory Nazianzen," *Tyndale Bulletin* 49.1 (1998), 155–157.

Ἕβδομον, ὗσε χάλαζα μέση πυρὸς, ὄμβρος ἄμικτος.
10   Ὄγδοον, ἐξ ἀκρίδος ὤλετο χλωρὸν ἅπαν.
Εἴνατον, Αἰγύπτοιο πέδον κατὰ νὺξ ἐκάλυψε
Πρωτοτόκων δὲ μόρος ἡ δεκάτη βάσανος.

I.1.15. Ἡ τοῦ Μωϋσέως Δεκάλογος. (PG 37.476–477)

Τοὺς δὲ νόμους ἐχάραξε Θεὸς δέκα ἕν ποτε πλαξὶ
Λαϊνέαις· σὺ δέ μοι ἔγγραφε τῇ κραδίῃ.
Οὐ γνώσῃ Θεὸν ἄλλον, ἐπεὶ σέβας οἷον ἑνός γε.
Οὐ στήσεις ἴνδαλμα κενὸν, καὶ ἄπνοον εἰκώ.
5   Οὔ ποτε μαψιδίως μνήσῃ μεγάλοιο Θεοῖο.   [477]
Σάββατα πάντα φύλασσε μετάρσια καὶ σκιόεντα.
Ὄλβιος, ἢν τοκέεσσι φέρῃς χάριν, ἢν ἐπέοικε.
Φεύγειν ἀνδροφόνον παλάμης ἄγος, ἀλλοτρίης τε
Εὐνῆς, κλεπτοσύνην τε κακόφρονα, μαρτυρίαν τε
10   Ψευδῆ, ἀλλοτρίων τε πόθον, σπινθῆρα μόροιο.

The seventh, hail fell amidst the fire, an untempered downpour
    (Ex 9.13–35).
10 And eighth, everything green was devoured by locusts
    (Ex 10.1–20).
Ninth, night veiled the Egyptian plain (Ex 10.21–29).
And the tenth trial was the death of the first-born
    (Ex 11.1–12.36).

I.1.15. The Decalogue of Moses (PG 37.476–477)

God once inscribed these Ten Commandments on marble
    tablets
but You write them on my heart:
You shall not know another God, since you honor only one
    (Ex 20.3; Deut 5.7).
You shall not erect an empty façade, a lifeless image
    (Ex 20.4–6; Deut 5.8–10).
5 You shall never mention the lofty God in vain
    (Ex 20.7; Deut 5.11).
Observe every Sabbath; both the celestial and the shadowy
    (Ex 20.8–11; Deut 5.12–15).
Blessed are you if you do homage to your parents, as is right
    (Ex 20.12; Deut 5.16).
Flee the guilt of a murderous hand (Ex 20.13; Deut 5.17), and of
    another's
marriage bed (Ex 20.14; Deut 5.18), evil-minded theft
    (Ex 20.15; Deut 5.19), and false
10 witness (Ex 20.16; Deut 5.20); and desire for what belongs to
    others (Ex 20.17; Deut 5.21) is the spark of death.

I.1.13. Πατριάρχαι υἱοὶ τοῦ Ἰακώβ. (PG 37.475)

Δώδεκα δ' ἐξ Ἰακὼβ πατρὸς μεγάλοιο πάτραρχοι·
Ῥουβεὶμ, καὶ Συμεὼν, καὶ Λευὶ, τοῖς δ' ἔπ' Ἰούδας.
Αὐτὰρ ἔπειτα νόθοι, Δὰν, Νεφθαλεὶμ, Γάδ τε Ἀσήρ τε·
Αὖθις δ' εὐγενέες μνηστῶν ἄπο, Ἰσσάχαρ ἦεν,
Ζαβουλὼν, καὶ Ἰωσὴφ, καὶ πύματος Βενιαμίν.

I.1.19. Μαθηταὶ τοῦ Χριστοῦ ΙΒ. (PG 37.488)

Δώδεκα δ' αὖ Χριστοῖο Θεοῦ μεγάλοιο μαθηταί.
Πέτρος τ' Ἀνδρείας τε, Ἰωάννης τ', Ἰάκωβος.
Πέμπτος δ' ἦε Φίλιππος· ὁ δ' ἔκτος, Βαρθολομαῖος,
Ματθαῖος, Θωμᾶς τε, καὶ Ἀλφαίου Ἰάκωβος·
Ἰούδας τε, Σίμων τε, καὶ οὐ φατὸς ἄλλος Ἰούδας.

I.1.18. Περὶ τῆς τοῦ Χριστοῦ γενεαλογίας. (PG 37.480–487)

Ματθαῖος πόθεν, εἰπὲ, μέγας, Λουκᾶς τε φέριστος,
Τὴν μὲν ὅγ', αὐτὰρ ὁ τήνδε βίβλοις ἐνέθηκε γενέθλην,   [481]

I.1.13. The patriarchs, the sons of Jacob (PG 37.475)

Twelve are the forefathers, born of Jacob, the great father:
Ruben and Simeon and Levi, and, in addition to them, Judas
    (Gen 29.31–35);
and then after them the bastards, Dan, Naphtali (Gen 30.4–8),
    Gad and Asher (Gen 30.9–12).
And, again, the noble ones born of the betrothed spouses, were
    Issachar,
Zabulon (Gen 30.17–20), and Joseph (Gen 30.23) and, last,
    Benjamin (Gen 35.18).

I.1.19. The disciples of Christ (PG 37.488)

Twelve were the disciples of Christ the great God:
Peter and Andrew and John and James.
Fifth was Philip. Sixth, Bartholomew,
Matthew, and Thomas. Then James son of Alphaeus.
And Jude, and Simon. Then the other Judas not to be
    mentioned.

I.1.18. On the genealogy of Christ (PG 37.480–487)[5]

Tell me, how did the great Matthew insert one version of the
    Lineage
in the Scriptures and the noble Luke another,

[5]Palla, "Ordinamento e polimetria," 179, shows that this lengthy poem, preserved in Group III, is in fact composed of two different poems. The first, I.1.18A, comprises ll.1–59 and is primarily concerned to reconcile the genealogy of Matthew with that of Luke. The second, I.1.18B, comprises ll.60–102, and reports the genealogy according to Luke, in reverse order, and then, concisely, that of Matthew. To reconcile the genealogies, Gregory relies heavily on the account given by Julius Africanus, as preserved in Jerome's *De viris illustribus* (63.3). Palla also notes the variety in the poem's meter, which may have fostered memorization. Indentation signals a metrical shift.

Αἳ Χριστὸν κατάγουσιν ἀφ' αἵματος ἀρχεγόνοιο;
Πῶς δ' ὁ μὲν ἐν πλεόνεσσιν, ὅδ' ἐν παύροισιν ἔληξεν;
5   Ἐς Δαυῒδ μὲν ἄνακτα γένους ῥόος ἀμφοτέροισιν
Ἄτμητος· μετέπειτα ῥέει δίχα, ὑστάτιον δὲ
Συμφέρεθ' ὡς ἐπὶ πόντον ἀπείρονα Χριστὸν ὁδεύων.
Ὧδέ κεν ἀθρήσειας, ἐμῷ δ' ἐπιπείθεο μύθῳ·
Δαυΐδαι, Σολομών τε, Νάθαν τ' ἔσαν, ὧν ὁ μὲν εἷλκεν
10 Ὥς τε ῥόον μεγάλου ποταμοῦ, βασιλήϊον αἷμα·
Αὐτὰρ ὅγ' εὐαγέων τε φαεινοτάτων θ' ἱερήων.
Χριστὸς δ' ἀμφότερ' ἔσκεν, ἄναξ μέγας, ἀρχιερεύς τε.
Τοὔνεκα Ματθαῖος μὲν ἐγράψατο πνεύματι θείῳ
Τοὺς Σολομωντιάδας, Λουκᾶς δ' ἐς Νάθαν ὄρουσεν.
15 Ἐκ δὲ δύω γενεῶν, τῆς μὲν πλέον, ἐξ ἑτέρης δὲ   [482]
Παυρότερον τὸ ῥέεθρον ἐπελθέμεν· οὐ μέγα θαῦμα.
Οὐ μὲν παυρότερον· γενεῶν δ' οὐκ ἴσον ἀριθμόν.
Ὧδε τὰ πρῶτα κέασθεν, ἔπειτα δὲ εἰς ἓν ἄγερθεν.
Φράζε δὲ καὶ τόδε μοι, πατέρων δύο πῶς ποτ' Ἰωσήφ.
20 Τέθμιον ἦν Μωσῆος, ἐπὴν ἄσπερμος ὄληται
Ἑβραῖος, κάσιν ἤ τιν' ὀλωλότος, ἤ τινα πηῶν
Ἐγγύθεν, αἶψα δάμαρτα φίλην καὶ κτῆσιν ἔχοντα,
Σπερμαίνειν φθιμένῳ τε γόνον καὶ οἶκον ἀέξειν,
Ὄφρα κε μὴ νώνυμος ἐν ἀνθρώποισιν ὄληται.

which trace Christ from a first parent's blood?
How did the former count by many ancestors, while the latter
    by few?
5   Until King David, the Lineage's flow in both cases
is unbroken. Afterwards its flow splits, but then reunites in the
    end,
so that it leads to Christ, the boundless sea.
Thus take heed, and be convinced by my account:
the sons of David were Solomon and Nathan, the first who
    drew
10 the royal blood as though a stream from a great river;
the latter was one of the holy and most brilliant priests.
But Christ claimed both ancestors, as a great king and a high
    priest.
Therefore Matthew, inspired by God the Spirit, wrote of the
    sons of
Solomon, while Luke rushed up to Nathan.
15 From the two lineages, the one grander, the other
smaller, we come upon the flowing stream. No great wonder.
For the second isn't really smaller; rather the number of the
    generations isn't the same.[6]
Thus the first generations split, but then they are gathered into
    one.
But tell me this as well, how can Joseph be the son of two
    fathers?
20 There was a law of Moses that when a Hebrew died
sonless, some brother of the dead man or one
near to him in kinship, straightway took his dear wife and his
    property,
and begot a child for the dead and added to his house,
so that his name might not perish among humanity.[7]

---

[6]Gregory seems to mean that Matthew and Luke report the same genealogies, but Luke reports fewer additions to the generations (such as the names of the women).

[7]The "Levirate" marriage (cf. Deut 25.5–10), that is, if a married man dies childless, his brother should marry his widow.

25 Τοὔνεκα κρυπτὸν ὕπερθε Θεοῦ βροτέου τόδ' ἀνεῦρον.
    Ματθὰν ἐκ Σολομῶνος ἄγων γένος, ἡγάγετ' Ἐσθάν.
    Τοῦ δ' ἄρ' ἀποφθιμένοιο, Ναθείδης οὔνομα Μελχί.   [483]
    Καὶ τῷ μὲν Ἰακὼβ, τῷ δ' Ἡλεὶ γείνατο παῖδας.
    Ἡλεὶ δὲ φθιμένοιο, ἐπεὶ γόνον οὔτιν' ἔλειπεν,
30 Αἶψα δόμον τε λέχος τε Ἰακὼβ οὐχ ὁμόπατρος
    Δέξατο, καὶ τέκεν υἱὸν ἀδελφεῷ ἐσθλὸν Ἰωσήφ.
    Οὕτω τοῦ μὲν ἔην, τῷ δ' ἔγραφε θεσμὸς Ἰωσήφ.
        Εὐαγγελιστῶν δ' ὃς μὲν εἶπε τὴν φύσιν,
        Ματθαῖος, ὃς δ' ἔγραψε Λουκᾶς τὸν νόμον.
35   Παῦσαι διοχλῶν τὴν καλὴν συμφωνίαν.
    Πῶς Δαυῒδ ἐς ἄνακτα φέρει Θεὸς, εὖτε φαάνθη
    Μητέρος ἐκ βροτέης Θεὸς ἄμβροτος· ἐκ μὲν Ἰωσὴφ,
    Πῶς ὅγε; παρθενικῆς γὰρ ἔην πάϊς, ἐκ Μαρίης δὲ,
    Λευίδης· Μαριὰμ γὰρ ἀφ' αἵματος ἦεν Ἀαρών.
40 Μάρτυς δ' ἄγγελος ἄμμιν, ἐπεὶ Προδρόμοιο γενέθλην   [484]
    Ἀγγέλλων μεγάλοιο φάους θεοειδέϊ μητρὶ,
    Μητέρας ἀμφοτέρας ὅγ' ἀνήγαγεν ἐς μέγαν Ἀαρών.
    Φρῆτραι δ' αὖ βασιλῆος ἀμιγέες, ἡ δ' ἱερήων.
    Οὐκ ἔτυμον. Φρῆτραι μὲν ἔσαν δίχα, πολλάκι δ' αὖτε
45 Μίγνυντο. Πρόσθεν μὲν Ἀρὼν μεγάλοιο θύγατρα
    Ἤγαγετ' ἐς μέγα δῶμα Ναασσὼν, ὃς δ' ἀπ' Ἰούδα

25 Thus I uncovered this, hidden above, within the Mortal God.
Matthan coming from the lineage of Solomon, married Estha.[8]
But when he died, a son of Nathan named Melchi married her,
she bore a son Jacob to Matthan, and a son Heli to Melchi.
But when Heli died, since he left no offspring,

30 Jacob, even though of a different father
immediately took his home and begot a prized son Joseph for
      his brother.
In this way Joseph would be his [i.e., Jacob's], but the law would
      assign him to the other [i.e, Heli].
    So of the evangelists Matthew spoke about nature
    but Luke spoke about the Law.

35   Stop dissecting the lovely harmony.
How did God bring him to King David, since
the immortal God appeared from the mortal mother? And
      from Joseph,
how does this work? For he was the son of a virgin, from Mary,
a Levite. For Mary was from the blood of Aaron.

40 An angel is a witness for us, when, proclaiming the birth of the
      Forerunner,
at lofty light, to the godlike mother (Lk 1.36),
he traced both mothers back to great Aaron.
The king's tribe might seem unmixed, so too the priests',
but that's not true. For though the tribes divided, they often

45 mixed again. Once Nahshon, who was sixth in descent from
      Judah
took the daughter of great Aaron into his lofty home.[9]

[8] For this problem Eusebius (*Historia Ecclesiastica* 1.7) also has a long discussion, which Gregory seems to adopt here. But Eusebius seems to rely on the claim that "Melchi" was Christ's grandfather, whereas both Gospels read "Matthat." Palla notes that the names were often conflated ("Ordinamento e polimetria," 180; cf. Ambrose, *In Lucam* 3.15).

[9] According to Ex 6.23, Aaron, a Levite, married Elisheba, who was sister of Nahshon, who was of the tribe of Judah. I cannot find the reference to Nahshon marrying Aaron's daughter. Perhaps Gregory is confused about the details here, but even if he is wrong, the reference still proves that the tribes mixed.

Ἕκτος ἔην. Μετέπειτα δ' ἐπεὶ πόλιν ὤλεσεν αἰχμὴ
Ἀσσυρίων, Βαβυλών τε τὰ τέθμια πάντα τίναξεν,
Οὐδὲ φυλῶν τῆμόσδε διακριδὸν αἷμα φυλάχθη
50   Οὕτω μὲν διὰ μητρὸς ἀνέρχεται ἐς βασιλῆας.
Ἐκ δὲ πατρὸς δοκέοντος ὅπως, φράζεσθαι ἄνωγα.
Αὐγούστου βασιλῆος ἐπεὶ φόρος ἔγραφε πάντας
Ἄλλοι μέν τ' ἄλλησιν ἐνὶ πτολίεσσι γράφοντο   [485]
Πατρῴαις, Δαυῖδ δὲ φίλον πέδον αἶψα κίχανον
55   Βηθλεὲμ, ᾗ κόλποισι μέγαν ὑπεδέξατο Χριστὸν,
Ἀμφότεροι, μνηστή τε φίλη, καὶ κεδνὸς Ἰωσὴφ
Γραψόμενοι. Φρήτρης γὰρ ἰῆς ἔσαν. Ὧδ' ἐνὶ φάτνῃ
Μήτηρ παρθενικὴ, κόσμου τέκε παντὸς ἄνακτα.
[I.1.18B]   Οὕτω καὶ διὰ πατρὸς ἀνέρχεται ἐς βασιλῆας.

60   Ἔμπαλι μὲν γενεὴν Λουκᾶς μέγας ἤγαγε μύθῳ
Εἰς Ἀδὰμ ἐκ Χριστοῖο. Ἐμοὶ δ' Ἀδὰμ ἦλθ' ἐπὶ Χριστόν.
Χειρὶ Θεοῦ πρώτιστος Ἀδὰμ γένετ'. Ἐκ δ' Ἀδάμοιο
Σὴθ πέλε. Τοῦ δ' ἄρ' Ἐνώς. Τοῦ, τέτρατος ἦε Καϊνάν.
Τοῦ δ' ἦν Μαλελεήλ. Τοῦ δ' Ἰαρὲδ, ὃς τέκε παῖδα
65   Κεῖνον Ἐνὼχ, ὃς ζωὸς ἐς οὐρανὸν ἦλθεν ἀερθείς.
Τοῦδε, Μαθουσάλα ἔσκεν, ὃς υἱέα γείνατο Λάμεχ.
Αὐτὰρ ὅ, Νῶε πατήρ. Σὴμ, Νώεος υἱὸς ἐκείνου.
Ἐκ τοῦ δ' Ἀρφαξὰδ, Καϊνὰν, Σαλά· τοῦ δ' ἐνέπουσιν
Υἱὸν Ἔβερ. Ἔβερος δὲ Φάλεκ πάϊς. Ἐκ δ' ἄρα Φαλὲκ,
70   Ἔσκε Ῥαγάβ. Κεῖνος δὲ Σεροὺχ τέκεν, ὃς τέκε Ναχώρ.
Ἀβραὰμ αὖτ' ἐπὶ τοῖσδε, πάϊς Θάρα Ναχορίδαο.   [486]
Ἀβραμίδης δ' Ἰσαὰκ Ἰακὼβ τέκεν, ὃς δ' ἄρ' Ἰούδαν.
Αὐτὰρ ὃ ἐκ Θαμάρης Φαρὲς τέκεν. Αὐτὰρ ὅ, Ἐσρώμ.
Ἐσρώμ, τὸν Ἀρὰμ, ὃς τὸν Ἀμιναδάμ. Ὃς δὲ Νααςσών.

But later when the sword of the Assyrians
destroyed the city, and Babylon overturned all her laws,
no blood distinction of the tribes was thence observed.
50 Thus indeed one traces up to the kingship through the mother.
I bid you tell how this might lead from the apparent father.
Since when Augustus was king, the census inscribed all,
some were inscribed in others' paternal cities.
So they reached of a sudden the land dear to David,
55 Bethlehem, who received the great Christ in her bosom,
and both the lovely wedded one and the cherished Joseph
were inscribed. But they were from a single tribe. In this way a
    virgin mother
bore in a crib the ruler of all the world.
[I.1.18B] Thus he also traces up to the kingship through his father.[10]

60 In reverse the great Luke traced the genealogy in his account
up to Adam from Christ; Adam came to me through Christ.
Adam was first created by the hand of God. And from Adam
Seth was born. His son was Enosh. His fourth son was Kenan.
His was Mahalelel. His was Jared, who begot that son
65 Enoch, who, while alive, went raised up into heaven.
He had Methuselah, who begot the son Lamech.
He was the father of Noah. Then Shem, the son of that Noah.
Arphaxad was his, and Cainan, and Shelah. They say his son
    was Eber.
Peleg was the son of Eber. But from Peleg, came Ragab [Reu].
70 That one begot Serug, who begot Nahor.
Again, Abraham came from these, the son of Terah
    Nachorides.
Isaac son of Abraham begot Jacob, who begot Judah.
He then begot Perez from Thamares. And he begot Esrom.
Esrom, Aram, who begot Amenadam. Who begot Naasson.

[10]This line makes more sense if we take it as the conclusion of a separate poem;
Joseph, from Bethlehem, is from the royal line of David.

75 Νασσὼν δ' αὖ, Σαλμών. Σαλμὼν, Βοόζ. Ἐκ Βοὸζ, Ὠβήδ.
    Ὠβὴδ δ' Ἰεσσαί· τοῦ δ' ἐκ μέγας ἔπλετο Δαυΐδ.
    Δαυίδης δὲ, Νάθαν, ὃς Ματθὰν υἱὸν ἔτικτεν,
    Ὅς Μαϊνάν. Μαϊνὰν, Μελεὰν τέκε. Ὅς δ' Ἐλιακείμ.
    Ὅς τὸν Ἰωάναν. Ὅς τὸν Ἰωσήφ. Ὅς, τὸν Ἰούδαν
80 Γείνατο. Τοῦ, Συμεών. Τοῦ, Λευί. Τοῦ ἄπο, Ματθάν.
    Τοῦδε, Ἰωρείμ. Τοῦ δ' Ἐλιέζερ. Τοῦδε, Ἰωσάφ.
    Τοῦ δ' Ἧρ. Τοῦ δ' Ἐλμώδ. Τοῦ δ' αὖ πάϊς ἔπλετο Κωσάμ.
    Κωσὰμ, ἔην Ἀδδί. Τοῦ, Μελχί. Τοῦ δ' ἄπο, Νηρί.
    Τοῦ δ' ἄπο, Σαλαθιὴλ, Ζοροβάβελ, Ῥησὰ, Ἰωνὰν,
85 Ἰούδας, Ὡσώκ, Σεμεεί τ' αὖ, Ματθίας τε,
    Καὶ Μαὰθ, Ναγγαὶ, καὶ Ἐσλείμ· τοῦ δ' ἄπο Ναοὺμ,
    Ἀμὼς, Ματθαθίας, καὶ Ἰωσὴφ, ἠδὲ Ἰανναί·   [487]
    Μελχὶ, καὶ Λευὶ, καὶ Ματθὰν, Ἡλεὶ, Ἰωσήφ.
    Λουκᾶς μὲν οὕτω. Πῶς δὲ Ματθαῖος μέγας;
90 Ἐξ Ἀβραὰμ μὲν μέχρι Δαυΐδ, ὡς ἔφην.
    Ἔνθεν δὲ Λουκᾶ τὴν ἱερατικὴν παρεὶς
    Σπορὰν, τίθησι τοῦ γένους ἀνακτόρων.
    Εἰσὶν δ' ὅσοι τε καὶ τίνες, λελέξεται.
    Δαυίδης, Σολομών, Ῥοβοὰμ, Ἀβίας τε, Ἀσά τε.
95 Τοῦ δ' Ἰωσαφὰτ ἔσκεν. Ὁ δ' ἕβδομος ἦεν Ἰωράμ.
    Ὀζίας, ἠδ' Ἰωάθαμ, ἠδ' Ἄχαζ, Ἐζεκίας τε,
    Καὶ Μανασῆ, καὶ Ἀμὼς, Ἰωσίας. Αὐτὰρ ἔπειτα
    Ἰεχονίας, ἁλωτὸν ὃν ἤγαγον ἐς Βαβυλῶνα·
    Σαλαθιὴλ, Ζοροβάβελ, Ἀβιοὺδ, ἠδ' Ἐλιακεὶμ,
100 Ἀζώρ. Τοῦδε, Σαδώκ. Τοῦ δ' Ἀχίν. Τοῦ δ' Ἐλιούδα.
    Τοῦδ' Ἐλιέζερ ἔην. Τοῦ, Ματθάν. Τοῦ δὲ Ἰακώβ.
    Ὕστατος, ὃς δοκέεσκε πατὴρ Χριστοῖο, Ἰωσήφ.

75   Nasson again, Salmon, Salmon, Booz.
      From Booz, Obed. From Obed, Jesse. Of whom the great
           David was begotten.
      David begot Nathan, who begot a son Matthan.
      Who begot Mainan. Mainan begot Melean. Who begot
           Eliakeim.
      Who begot John. Who begot Joseph. Who begot
80   Judah. From him, Symeon. From him, Levi. From him
           Matthan.
      From him Joreim. From him Eliezer. From him Josaph.
      From him Er. From him Elmod. In turn from him a son
           Cosam was begotten.
      Addi was from Kosam. From him Melchi. From him Neri.
      From him Shealtiel, Zerubbabel, Rhesa, Joanan,
85   Joda, Josech, then Semein, Mattathias,
      and Maath, Naggai, and Esli. From him Nahum,
      Amos, Mattathias, and Joseph, and then Jannai.
      Melki, and Levi, and Matthat, Heli, Joseph.
      And so Luke. But how did great Matthew do it?
90   From Abraham until David, as I said.
      While in Luke you find the priestly
      strain, he established the genealogy of kings.
      However many and who they were, will now be told:
      Solomon son of David, Rehoboam, [the father of] Abijah. Asa
95   was the father of Jehoshaphat. But the seventh was Jehoram.
      Uzziah, then Jotham, then Ahaz, then Hezekiah,
      then Mannaseh, then Amon, and Josiah. But then
      Jeconiah, whom they led captive into Babylon.
      Shealtiel, Zerubbabel, Abiud, and Eliakim.
100   Azor, whose son was Zadok, whose son was Akim, whose son
           was Eliud
      whose son was Eleazar. Whose son was Matthan. Whose son
           was Jacob.
      And last, the apparent father of Christ, Joseph.

I.1.20. Τὰ τοῦ Χριστοῦ θαύματα κατὰ Ματθαῖον.
(PG 37.488–491)

Ματθείης βίβλοιο τὰ θαύματα, ὁππόσ' ἔρεξε
Χριστὸς ἄναξ βροτέῳ σώματι κιρνάμενος.
Πρῶτον μὲν λεπροῖο πικρὴν ἀπεσείσατο νοῦσον,
Εἶθ' ἑκατοντάρχου παιδὸς ἔπηξε μέλη.
5   Τὸ τρίτον αὖ Πέτρου ἑκυρῆς φλόγα ἔσβεσε χειρί.
Τέτρατον, οἶδμα μέγα εὔνασε καὶ ἀνέμους.
Δαίμονας ἧκε σύεσσι τὸ πέμπτον, ἐν Γεργεσσηνοῖς.   [489]
Ἕκτον, ἑὴν κλίνην ἧρε βαρὺς μέλεσιν.
Ἕβδομον, ἁψαμένης πηγὴν σχέθεν αἱμοροούσης.
10   Ἄρχοντος θυγάτηρ ὄγδοον εὗρε φάος.
Ἔνατον αὖ, τυφλοῖσι πόρεν φάος. Ἐκ δ' ἐλαθέντος
Δαίμονος, οὐ λαλέων ῥῆξε λόγον, δέκατον.
Σαββάτῳ ἑνδέκατον, ξηρὴν χέρα λύσατο δεσμῶν,
Ὄσσε δὲ δαιμονίου κ' οὔατα, δωδέκατον.
15   Ἐκ δεκάτοιο τρίτον, κοφίνους δυοκαίδεκα πλῆσε,
Κἀνδρῶν χιλιάδας πέντ' ἀπὸ πέντ' ἀκόλων.
Τέτρατον ἐκ δεκάτου δὲ, κιχήσατο νῆα πόδεσσι·
Τοῖς δ' ὑπόειξε μέγας πόντος ὀρινόμενος.
Πέντε δὲ καὶ δέκατον, Χαναναίας πνεῦμ' ἐδίωξε,

I.1.20. The miracles of Christ according to Matthew
(PG 37.488–491)[11]

The marvels of the book of Matthew, just so many as
Christ the king performed, mixed, in a mortal body.
First he shook off the painful illness of the leper (8.1–4).
Next he bound the limbs of the centurion's slave (8.5–13).
5   Then third he quenched the fever of Peter's mother-in-law by
      hand (8.14–15).
Fourth he calmed the great swell and the winds (8.23–26).
Fifth he cast the demons into swine at Gergesenes (8.28–34).
Sixth the man with withered limbs took up his litter (9.1–8).
Seventh he stopped the bleeding woman's flow when touched
      (9.20–22).
10 Eighth the ruler's daughter found the light (9.23–26).
And ninth he gave light to the blind (9.27–30). When his
      demon
was driven out, a dumb man spoke a word, the tenth (9.32–33).
Eleven, on the Sabbath, he freed a dry hand from its chains
      (12.9–13).
Twelfth he freed the eyes and ears of a man possessed (12.22).
15 Thirteenth he filled twelve baskets,
as well as five thousand men, from five bits [of bread]
      (14.13–21).
Fourteenth he reached the ship by foot;
the great and stormy sea withdrew from them (14.22–32).
Fifteenth he drove a spirit out of a Canaanite girl,

[11] According to Palla's reconstruction, this is the first in the series on the miracles and parables of Christ. As the opening poem, it is the longest of the group and most carefully fashioned; many of the details of the miracles present here are absent from the other poems. Although Gregory stops numbering the miracles at twenty, the final two miracles seem to count in the catalogue. If so, then we have twenty-two miracles, a nice mnemonic, where the number of miracles equals the number of books in the OT, which equals the number of letters in the Hebrew alphabet.

20   Μητρὶ χαριζόμενος πολλὰ λιταζομένῃ.
      Ἕκτον καὶ δέκατον, σπυρίδας λίπον ἕπτ᾽ ἀπὸ ἑπτὰ
      Ἄρτων, χιλιάδες τέσσαρες, ἥν τε κόρος.   [490]
      Ἑπτὰ δὲ καὶ δέκατον, θείην ἠλλάξατο μορφὴν,
      Στράψας οἷσι φίλοις ἠελίοιο πλέον.
25   Ὀκτωκαιδέκατον δὲ, σεληναίης ἀπὸ νούσου
      Ὡς ἱκέτευσε πατὴρ, λύσατο παῖδα φίλον.
      Ἐννεακαιδέκατον, φάος ὄμμασιν ἐξ Ἱεριχοῦς
      Τυφλοῖς εἰνοδίοις δῶκε πορευόμενος.
      Εἰκοστὸν δ᾽ αὐγὰς πόρεν ὄμμασι, πηρά τ᾽ ἔλυσε
30   Γούνατα, ἐξ ἱεροῦ λύματα πάντ᾽ ἐλάσας.
      Θαῦμα δὲ Βηθανίηθεν ἰὼν ποίησε μέγιστον,
      Ξηρὴν αἶψα συκῆν, ὥς μιν ἄκαρπον ἴδεν.
      Ἐκ δ᾽ ἐχύθη σταυροῖο βαθὺ σκότος, οἰχομένοιο
      Φωτὸς, καὶ νηοῦ εὐρὺ πέτασμα ῥάγη.
35   Γαῖα δὲ παλλομένη, γαίης ὕπερ ἔσχισε πέτρας,
      Καὶ νέκυες τύμβους λεῖψαν ἀνεγρόμενοι.
      Αὐτὰρ ὅγε τριτάτῳ ἐνὶ ἤματι τύμβον ἀνοίξας,   [491]
      Αὖθις ἑοῖσι φίλοις ἐν Γαλιλαί᾽ ἐφάνη.

20 pleasing her mother who begged him persistently (15.21–28).
Sixteenth four thousand men left seven baskets full
from seven loaves, while they were satisfied (15.32–38).
And seventeenth he altered his divine form,
shining to his friends more brightly than the sun (17.1–3).
25 Eighteenth, just as a father was begging him,
he freed his precious son from epilepsy (17.15–18).
Nineteenth as he headed from Jericho he gave sight to
the eyes of blind men traveling on the road (20.29–34).
Twentieth he gave sunlight to eyes; he freed
30 paralyzed knees (21.14); he drove all filth from the Temple
(21.12).
Leaving Bethany he did his greatest miracle:
the fig tree suddenly went sterile when he found it fruitless
(21.18–20).[12]
From the Cross a deep darkness flowed out, the light
vanished and the wide veil of the Temple was rent (27.45–51).
35 And the earth quivered, and above the rocky earth, it split
(27.51)
and the dead, aroused, abandoned their own tombs (27.52–53).
But then he opened the tomb on the third day (28.1–7),
and appeared again to his friends in Galilee (28.16).

[12]Gregory's claim that this is Christ's μέγιστον miracle is strange, especially since he is just about to present the Resurrection. Elsewhere in his poems Gregory offers other candidates for the title of μέγιστον θαῦμα, including for instance, in the poem "On the Soul" (I.1.8, l.47), the resurrection of the body. Here he may be claiming that the miracle is Christ's greatest because it signifies the passing away of the Old Law and the revelation of the New.

I.1.24. Τοῦ αὐτοῦ παραβολαὶ καὶ αἰνίγματα.
(PG 37.495–496)

Εἰ δ' ἄγε, καὶ σκοτίων αἰνίγματα δέρκεο μύθων·
Οἶκον ἐπὶ ψάμμου κείμενον ἀδρανέος,
Καὶ σπόρον, ὡς ἐπὶ γαῖαν ὁμοῖϊος, ἦλθεν ἄνισος·
Καὶ σπόρον, ᾧ καλῷ σπέρματα ἐχθρὰ μίγη·
5   Καὶ δένδρον, ὀλίγον νάπυος σπόρον· εἶτ' ἐν ἀλεύρῳ
Ζύμην κρυπτομένην· ὤνιον ἀγρὸν ἔτι
Θησαυροῖο χάριν· καὶ μαργαρίτην πολύτιμον,
Ἔμπορος ὃν πάντων ἐπρίατο κτεάνων·
Καὶ νεπόδων ἕλκουσαν ἅπαν γένος ἐξ ἁλὸς ἄρκυν·
10 Αἰρόμενόν τ' ὤμοις πλαζόμενον πρόβατον·
Καὶ πικρῷ θεράποντι χρέους πέρι, πικρὸν ἄνακτα
Καὶ πρώτοις πυμάτους μισθὸν ἔχοντας ἴσον·
Πεμπομένους θ' υἱῆας ἐς ἄμπελον οὐδὲν ὁμοίους,   [496]
Καὶ τοὺς κληρονόμον ὠσαμένους θανάτῳ·
15 Καὶ σχεδίους νυμφῶνι φίλην πλήσαντας ἑορτήν·
Ἔνθεν ἀκοιμήτους ἐν δαΐδεσσι κόρας
Καὶ κύριον δούλοισι νέμοντ' οὐκ ἴσα τάλαντα·
Ἔμπαλιν αὖ προβάτοις ἱσταμένους ἐρίφους.

I.1.24. The parables and puzzles according to Matthew
(PG 37.495–496)[13]

Come then, and consider the puzzles of the darkened words:
the house built on unstable sand (7.24–27),
the seed, though cast the same upon the earth, grows unequally
  (13.1–8).
And the seed, though good, to which bad seeds were mixed
  (13.24–30).
5   The shrub, a little seed of mustard (13.31–32). Then the yeast
hidden in the dough (13.33). A field purchased
for the sake of its treasure (13.44). And the pearl of great price,
which the merchant bought for all he owned (13.45–46);
dragging the net from the sea with all sorts of fish (13.47–48).
10   Taking the lost sheep on his shoulders (18.10–14).
And the king who was harsh to his servant, petty about his
  debts (18.21–35).
The last ones who earn pay equal to those who were first
  (20.1–16).
The sons, who were nothing alike, sent into the vineyard
  (21.28–32).
And those who threw the heir out to his death (21.33–43).
15   And the last-minute guests who filled the feast beloved by the
  groom (22.1–13).
And then the virgins making vigil with the torches (25.1–13).
And the master who gave his slaves unequal talents (25.14–30).
And the sheep and the goats set up in opposition (25.31–46).

---

[13]The syntax of the poem is rather difficult, even more than in the poem on the miracles, since the details of the parables are almost entirely ignored. Only a reader who was already quite familiar with the Gospel text could make out the sequence of references, and even then ambiguities remain.

I.1.20. Τὰ Χριστοῦ θαύματα κατὰ Μάρκον. (PG 37.491–492)

Μάρκος δ' Αὐσονίοισι Θεοῦ τάδε θαύματ' ἔγραψε,
Πέτρῳ θαρσαλέος Χριστοῦ μεγάλῳ θεράποντι.
Δαίμων καὶ πυρετὸς, καὶ λέπρη, καὶ παράλυσις
Εἶξε λόγῳ Χριστοῦ. Μετέπειτα δὲ χεὶρ ἐτανύσθη
5   Ξηρή· καὶ ἀνέμων λῆξεν μένος ἠδὲ θαλάσσης.
Καὶ λεγεὼν ὑπόειξε, καὶ αἱματόεσσαν ἔπαυσε
Πηγὴν, καὶ θυγατρὶ ζωὴν πόρ' Ἰαείροιο.
Πέντε δ' ἄρ' ἐξ ἄρτων πολλοὶ τράφεν. Ἔνθεν ἔδησε
Πόντον ἐπιστείβων. Μετέπειτα δὲ, πνεῦμ' ἐδίωξε
10   Φοινίσσης, Τυρίοισι τέρας καὶ Σιδονίοισι,
Κωφόν τ' οὐ λαλέον. Θρέψεν πάλιν ἔπτ' ἀκόλοισιν   [492]
Ἀνδρῶν χιλιάδας· καὶ τυφλὸς ἴδεν φάος. Εἶτα
Καὶ μορφῆς ἀπέπεμψε σέλας, καὶ δεσμὸν ἔλυσε
Γλώσσης, πνεῦμ' ἐλάσας· Βαρτιμαῖός τε φάοσδε
15   Τυφλὸς ἐξ Ἰεριχοῦντος ἐσέδρακεν. Ὡς δὲ ἄκαρπον
Εὗρε συκῆν χατέων, νεκρὰν ἔθηκε λόγῳ.
Τυφλοὺς δ' αὖ χωλούς τε ἰήσατο ἐγγύθι νηοῦ.

I.1.21. The miracles of Christ according to Mark (PG 37.491–492)

Mark wrote these miracles of God for the Ausonians,
relying on Peter, the great servant of Christ.[14]
The demon-possessed, fever, leprosy, and paralysis
are healed upon the word of Christ (1.21–2.12). And then a man
    has dried
5   hands restored (3.1–5). He calmed the wrath of storms and sea
    (4.35–41);
Legion obeyed (5.1–5.10); he stopped the hemorrhaging
wound (5.24–34); then he gave life to Jairus' daughter (5.35–42).
Many ate from a mere five loaves (6.30–44); then he subdued
    the sea
by treading on it (6.45–49). And he drove a spirit
10   from a Phoenician girl (7.24–30), so that Tyre and Sidon were
    in awe;[15]
he made the dumb to speak (7.31–37). He fed thousands of men
from seven bits of bread (8.1–8). The blind man saw (8.22–26).
    And then
his bright form shone out (9.2–8). And then he loosed the
    chain
that bound the tongue, driving out the spirit (9.26–27).
    Bartimaeus the blind man
15   from Jericho looked upon the light (10.46–52). When hungry,
    he found no figs
on the tree, so he spoke and made it die (11.12–14).
In Temple precincts, he healed the blind and lame.[16]

---

[14]Gregory reprises the attribution he makes in I.1.12, where he writes that Mark "wrote the marvels of Christ for Italy."

[15]The last seven lines of the poem are corrupt; although they are printed as hexameters in the PG, the manuscripts present them variously as elegiacs or in mixed meter; see Palla, "Ordinamento e polimetria," 183.

[16]The reference is unclear. At Mk 11.15–17 Jesus drives the moneychangers from the Temple precincts.

I.1.25. Παραβολαὶ Χριστοῦ κατὰ Μάρκον. (PG 37.496–497)

Τόσσα Χριστὸς ἔρεξε μέγας, μύθους δ' ἀγόρευσε
Παρβλήδην· ἐπὶ γαῖαν ἕνα σπόρον οὔτι ὅμοιον,
   Καὶ τὸν ζιζανίων σπέρματι συμφυέα,
   Καὶ νάπυ, κληρονόμον τε θανόνθ' ὑπὸ χερσὶν ἀθέσμοις.
5 Μάρκος μὲν δὴ τοῖα, Πέτρου φυτόν· εὐρυχόρῳ δὲ
   Ἑλλάδι Παύλοιο Λουκᾶς ἔγραψε τάδε·   [497]
Δαίμων, καὶ πυρετὸς, καὶ ἄγρη, λέπρα, λύσις τε.

I.1.22. Τοῦ αὐτοῦ θαύματα κατὰ Λουκᾶν. (PG 37.492–494)

Λουκᾶς δ' Ἑλλάδι σεπτὰ Θεοῦ τάδε θαύματ' ἔγραψε,
Παύλῳ θαρσαλέος Χριστοῦ μεγάλῳ θεράποντι.
Δαίμων καὶ πυρετὸς καὶ λέπρη καὶ παράλυσις
Εἶξε λόγῳ· καὶ χεὶρ τείνατο καρφαλέη.
5 Εἶθ' ἑκατοντάρχοιο λελυμένον ἥδρασε παῖδα·
Χήρῃ τ' ἐκ νεκύων ἐν Ναῒμ υἷα πόρε.   [493]
Τὴν δὲ μύρῳ χρίσασαν ἁγνοὺς πόδας ἥγνισε μύθῳ.
Καὶ στῆσεν ἀνέμους, καὶ λεγεῶνα μέγαν.

I.1.25. Parables of Christ according to Mark (PG 37.496–497)[17]

> Great Christ performed many deeds, proclaiming stories
>> in parable form. On earth one planting is not the same
>> (4.1–9).
>> [Although planted together with the seed of the weeds
>> (4.26–29).]
> And the mustard seed (4.30–32), and the heir killed by the
>> lawless hands (12.1–12).
> 5 [Mark recorded these things, the offshoot of Peter. Luke
>> wrote this
> for Paul's wide-ranging Hellas:
>> the demon, and the fever, and the field, the leprosy, and
>> the purification]

I.1.22. The miracles according to Luke (PG 37.492–494)

> Luke wrote these splendid miracles of God for Greece,
> relying on Paul, the great servant of Christ.
> A demon (4.31–35) and a fever (4.38–39) and leprosy (5.12–15)
>> and paralysis (5.17–25)
> yielded at his word. And the dried hand stretched forth
>> (6.6–10).
> 5 Then he settled the ailing servant of the centurion (7.1–10).
> He gave the widow at Nain her son back from the dead
>> (7.11–16).
> By his word he purified her who anointed his pure feet with
>> ointment (7.46–48).
> He settled both the winds (8.22–25) and that great Legion
>> (8.26–31).

---

[17]From the manuscript evidence, Palla claims that only lines 1, 2, and 4 of this poem as it is printed in the PG are authentic. If so, there is very little content to the verse, a mere three parables.

Αἵματος ἔσχε ῥύσιν, καὶ Ἰαείροιο θύγατρα
10   Ἤγαγεν ἐς ζωήν. Πέντε δ᾽ ἄρ᾽ ἐξ ἀκόλων
Καὶ δύο ἰχθυδίων, ἐν ἐρήμῳ πέντε ποτ᾽ ἀνδρῶν
Θρέψεν χιλιάδας. Εἴδεος ἦκε σέλας.
Δαίμονα τηλυγέτοιο πικρὸν ἀποέργαθε παιδὸς,
Καὶ τὸν ἐπὶ γλώσσης ἥμενον, ὡς δὲ πάλαι
15   Ἑβραίην στυγερῇ νούσῳ κλίναντα γυναῖκα,
Ναὶ μὴν καὶ ὑδέρου ὄγκον ἀπεσκέδασε.
Καὶ λεπροὺς ἐκάθηρε δέκα, τῶν εἷς Σαμαρείτης.
Τυφλῷ τ᾽ ἐξ Ἱεριχοῦς φῶς πόρεν εἰνοδίῳ.
Ὅσσα τ᾽ ἀποψύχοντος ἴδον σημήϊα Χριστοῦ,
20   Ἠδ᾽ ὡς ἐκ νεκύων οἷσι φίλοισι φάνη.   [494]

I.1.26. Παραβολαὶ κατὰ Λουκᾶν. (PG 37.497–498)

Παροιμιῶν δὲ Λουκᾶς ἐμνήσθη τόσων·
Τοῦ θέντος ἕδραν ἀσφαλῆ πέτρης ὕπερ
Καὶ τοῦ παθόντος εὖ πλέον, καὶ τῷ πλέον
Στέργοντος· εἶτα τοῦ σπόρου εἰς τέσσαρας
5   Φύσεις πεσόντος γῆς· ἔπειθ᾽ ὁδοιπόρου
Λησταῖς πεσόντος. Εἶτ᾽ ἀωρὶ πρὸς θύρας
Ἐλθών τις αἰτεῖ, κ᾽ οὐ πονηρὰ λαμβάνει.
Ἀκάθαρτον εἶτα πνεῦμα δ᾽ εἰσοικίζεται
Ἑπτὰ ξὺν ἄλλοις. Καὶ μάτην τις ἐλπίσι
10   Καρπῶν γέγηθεν, ἀγνοῶν οἷ στήσεται.
Ἐκ τῶν γάμων δ᾽ ἥκοντι γρηγορητέον   [498]

And he held back the flow of blood (8.43–47), and he brought
    Jairus' daughter
10   into life (8.49–55). And from five loaves and two
fishes in the desert he once fed five-thousand
men (9.10–16). He showed the brilliance of his form (9.28–36).
He drove the evil demon from the only-born son (9.37–42),
likewise the one inhabiting another's mouth (11.14), just as
15   he drove off the one that long crippled the Hebress with a
    dread disease (13.10–16);
and once he cast the burden from a dropsied man (14.1–5).
And he cured ten lepers, one of them a Samaritan (17.11–19).
He gave sight to a blind man on the road from Jericho
    (18.35–43).
So many more signs they witnessed from the Christ (who
    passed away)
20   once he appeared from the dead, to his friends.

I.1.26. Parables according to Luke (PG 37.497–498)

So many parables did Luke record:
of him who set a firm seat built on rock (6.46–49)
and the one who loves more, because he has
suffered more (6.27–39). Then the seed falling on the four
5   kinds of the earth (8.4–8). Then the wayfarer
who falls in with thieves (10.25–37). Then he who comes quite
    early
to the door, begging; yet even he does not receive bad things
    (11.5–13).
And the unclean spirit entering to dwell
with seven others (11.26). And the one who vainly rests
10   in hopes of fruit, not knowing what will remain for him
    (12.13–21).
He who kept watch for the Anointed coming from

Χριστῷ, καλῶς τε τῇ θεραπείᾳ χρηστέον.
Συκῆν τ' ἄκαρπον ταῖς κόπροις ἐπωφελεῖν.
Νάπυ, ζύμη τε, καὶ πένητες ἐν γάμῳ.
15   Χαρά τε δραχμῆς εὑρέσει, καὶ θρέμματος.
Πατήρ τε παίδων τῷ πεσόντι συμπαθής.
Εἶτ' οἰκονόμος τι τῶν χρεῶν χαρίζεται
Κλέπτων προμηθῶς. Λάζαρος καὶ πλούσιος.
Ἐκεῖθε χήρας ἀξίωσις εὔτονος.
20   Εἶτ' αὖ Τελώνης, καὶ Φαρισσαίου τύφος.
Καὶ μνῶν μερισμὸς, ἰσάριθμος τοῖς δέκα.
Κακοὶ γεωργοὶ καὶ φονεῖς τοῦ δεσπότου.

I.1.23. Τοῦ αὐτοῦ θαύματα κατὰ Ἰωάννην. (PG 37.494)

Παῦρα δ' Ἰωάννου δήεις ἱερῇ ἐνὶ βίβλῳ
Θαύματα δὴ, πολλοὺς δὲ λόγους Χριστοῖο ἄνακτος.
Ἦν γάμος, οἰνοχόοι δ' ἐκέρων ἐξ ὕδατος οἶνον.
Εἶπε, καὶ υἱὸς ἄνουσος ἔην κάμνων βασιλίσκου.
5   Εἶπε, λέχος δ' ἀνάειρεν, ὃς οὐ φύγε δεσμὰ λοετροῖς.
Πέντε δ' ἔπειτ' ἄρτων τέλεσεν τέρας. Ἔνθεν ὅδευσεν
Πόντον ὑπερζείοντα, καὶ ἐξεσάωσε μαθητάς.
Τυφλὸν δ' ἐκ γενετῆς ἰήσατο, πηλὸν ἀλείψας.
Τέτρατον ἦμαρ ἔην καὶ Λάζαρος ἔγρετο τύμβου.

the wedding, a boon for one who ministers well (12.35–40);
the aiding of the fruitless fig with manure (13.6–8).
Mustard (13.18–19), and leaven (13.20–21), and the needy at the
wedding (14.15–24).
15 The joy in finding the drachma (15.8–10), and the nursling
(15.1–7).
And the father sympathetic to the son who fell (15.11–32).
And the steward congratulates the clever thieves who stole
his goods (16.1–13). Lazarus and the rich man (16.19–31).
And then a strict repayment of the widow (18.1–8).
20 Again the tax collector and the blindness of the Pharisee
(18.9–14),
and the dividing of the *menas* equally among the ten (19.11–27);
the evil farmers who were jealous of their master (20.9–19).

I.1.23. The miracles of Christ according to John (PG 37.494)

Now in the sacred book of John you will find few
marvels, but many words of Christ the king.
There was the wedding, and winepourers poured wine from
water (2.1–9).
He spoke, and the ill son of the official was made healthy
(4.43–50).
5 He spoke, and he who could not flee his chains, once cleansed
took up his bed (5.1–9).
Then he performed a miracle from five loaves (6.1–13). He then
traveled
over the turbulent sea, and rescued the disciples (6.16–21).
He healed the man who was blind from birth, anointing him
with mud (9.1–6).
On the fourth day, Lazarus was raised from the tomb
(11.17–44).

10   Αὐτὰρ ὁ καὶ νεκύεσσι θάνεν, καὶ ζῶσιν ἀναστὰς
      Χριστὸς ἄναξ ἀναφανδὸν ὁμίλεεν οἷς ἑτάροισι.

I.1.27. Παραβολαὶ τῶν τεσσάρων εὐαγγελιστῶν.
(PG 37.498–506)

      Δείδω μὴ βιότοιο θεμείλιον ἐν ψαμάθοισι
      Βαλλόμενος, ποταμοῖσι καὶ εἰν ἀνέμοισι κεδασθῶ,   [499]
      Ἢ σπόρος ὡς ἐπὶ γαῖαν ἰὼν ξηρὴν καὶ ἄκαρπον,
      Ὦκα μὲν ἀντείλαιμι, τάχιστα δὲ αὖος ἔοιμι,
5   Ἠελίοιο βολῇσι τυπείς, καὶ πήμασι τυτθοῖς·
      Ἢ με φάγοι πετεηνὰ, καὶ ἐκθλίψειαν ἄκανθαι.
      Μὴ δέ μοι ὑπνώοντι κακὸν σπόρον ἐγκαταμίξῃ
      Ζιζανίων ἀρότης τε κακῶν, καὶ βάσκανος ἐχθρός.
      Μὴ δ᾽ ἄρ᾽ ὁμοῦ χλοάουσι βαλὼν ἐπὶ χεῖρα φυτοῖσιν
10   Ἐσθλοῖς ἠδὲ κακοῖσι, πρὶν ἐν σταχύεσσι σταθῆναι,
      Σύν που ζιζανίοισι καλὸν φυτὸν ἐξολέσαιμι.
      Παύρων γὰρ τοιοῖσδε νοήμονα χεῖρ᾽ ἐπιθεῖναι,
      Ἔνθ᾽ ἀρετὴ κακίη τε διάνδιχα ναιετάουσαι,
      Ἀγχίθυροι γεγάασι, κακὸν δ᾽ ἐπιτέλλεται ἐσθλῷ.
15   Αἰνῶ τὸν ὀλίγον νάπυος σπόρον, ὡς ὀλίγος μὲν,
      Δενδροῦται δὲ τάχιστα, καὶ ἐς τόσον ὕψος ὁδεύει,
      Ὥστε καὶ ὀρνίθεσσι πέλειν σκέπας ἠερίοισι.   [500]
      Μάργαρε τιμήει καὶ κύδιμε, σοῦ δ᾽ ἄρ᾽ ἔγωγε
      Κάλλεος ἱμείρων, μέγας ἔμπορος αἴθε γενοίμην,
20   Πάντων δ᾽ ὅσσα μοί ἐστι μέχρις πυμάτοιο χιτῶνος.

10   And indeed he died for the dead, and, when he rose for the
           living
      Christ the king also appeared to his companions, conversing
           (20–21).

I.1.27. The parables of the four Gospels (PG 37.498–506)[18]

      I fear I am placing the foundation of my life on
      sand, and I am scattered in the seas and in the winds,
      or seed that falls on dry and sterile earth,
      though swiftly I shoot up, quickly I wither,
5   struck by the rays of sunlight, and by little blows;
      or a bird would eat me, and then thorns strangle me.
      And let not the sower of evil weeds, the jealous enemy,
      mix in evil seed while I sleep.
      And let me not lay my hand to the good
10   and evil shoots of grass alike, before the sprouts mature,
      lest I somehow destroy the good shoot with the weeds.
      For very few can put a knowing hand to these,
      where vice and virtue dwell apart,
      yet grow up together, evil is forced upon the good.
15   I praise the little mustard seed, though starting small,
      soon branches out, and grows to such a height,
      that it may offer perch for birds that dwell in air.
      O pearl, so honored and esteemed, I too,
      desirous of your beauty, would play the great merchant,
20   and all I have, up to my final tunic,

      [18]As discussed in the introduction, where one would expect the parables of John
we instead get Gregory's "final prayer." Here Gregory reexamines the Gospel parables,
often from a moral or a personal perspective, generally presenting them in six-line
units. Thirty-one lines of this poem appear in another of Gregory's verses, "Exhorta-
tion to virgins" (I.2.2); see Palla, "Ordinamento e polimetria," 184. On the latter poem,
see *Gregor von Nazianz: Mahnungen an die Jungfrauen (Carmen 1,2,2)*, commentary by
Frank E. Zehles and María José Zamora (Paderborn: Ferdinand Schöningh, 1996).

Ὤνιον ἀντιλάβοιμι φίλον κτέαρ, ὥς κεν ἅπαντας
Πλούτῳ νηκήσαιμι, πεπασμένος οἷον ἀπ' ἄλλων,
Ἢ θησαυρὸν ἀγροῖο μυχοῖς ἔνι κρυπτὸν ἐόντα!
Οἶδα δ' ἐγὼ καὶ κόσμον ἔσω πίπτοντα σαγήνης,
25   Ὧι Χριστοῦ βασιλῆος ὑποδρήσσοντες ἐφετμαῖς,
Ἀνθρώπων ἁλιῆες ἑὸν λίνον ἀμφὶς ἔθηκαν,
Ὡς ἁλὸς ἐξερύσωσι βυθῶν, ὁπάσωσι δὲ Χριστῷ
Νηχομένους πικροῖς ἐνὶ κύμασι τοῦδε βίοιο.
Ἀλλ' ὁπόταν κρίνῃς ἁλίην, διὰ δ' ἄνδιχα τέμνῃς,
30   Μή μ' ἀπὸ τῆλε βάλοις, ἀχρήϊον οἷά περ ἰχθύν·
Ἄγγεσι δ' ἐγκατάθειο φυλασσόμενον βασιλῆϊ.   [501]
Ἐς μεγάλην δὲ Θεοῖο καλὴν ἐριθηλέ' ἀλωήν,
Ἠῶος μὲν ἔβην, καὶ πλείονα μόχθον ἀνέτλην·
Μισθὸν δ' ὑστατίοισιν ἴσον, καὶ κῦδος ἔχοιμι.
35   Τίς φθόνος, εἰ μόχθοισι πόθον Θεὸς ἀντιφερίζει;
Πέμπε πατὴρ υἷας ἐς ἄμπελον, ὡς κομέοιεν,
Τὸν πρότερον, πρότερον· ὁ δ' ἄρα πρόφρων ὑπέδεκτο,
Οὐ μὴν ἐξετέλεσσε πατρὸς πόθον, ὥσπερ ὑπέστη.
Αὐτὰρ ὅγ' οὐχ ὑπέδεκτο, καὶ ἐξετέλεσσεν ἐφετμὴν
40   Ὁπλότερος. Κρείσσων μὲν ἐμοὶ, γλυκίων δὲ τοκῆϊ
Ἀμφοτέρων, ὃς ἔδεκτο, καὶ ἐξετέλεσσεν ἐέλδωρ.
Κληρονόμον δ' ὀλέσαιεν, ὅσοι πυρὸς, ἐκτὸς ἀλωῆς.
Ἔστι γάμος, τὸν παιδὶ πατὴρ φίλος ἐσθλὸς ἀρίστῳ
Δαίνυσι καγχαλόων· τοῦδ' ἀντιάσαιμι ἔγωγε,
45   Τοῦδ' ἐγὼ ἀντιάσαιμι, καὶ ὃς φίλος ἐστὶν ἔμοιγε!   [502]
Μίμνοι δ' ἔκτοθι κεῖνος, ὅτις πρὸ γάμοιο τίθησιν

my precious property, I'd trade instead through sale, and would
    surpass
all men in wealth, possessing this one thing above all else,
that is, the treasure hidden in the crannies of the field.
I know as well the world that falls within the net,

25   which, on command from Christ the king, while sailing,
the fishers of men surround by casting out the net,
so as to drag them from the ocean depths, and bid those
swimming on the bitter waves of this life follow Christ.
But when you judge the catch, dividing it in half,

30   may you not cast me far away, as though a useless fish,
but place me safe in vessels, guarded by the king.
Into God's vineyard, lovely, flourishing and vast,
at dawn I entered to undertake a weighty task.
I have a salary the same as latecomers, and equal praise:

35   who's jealous, if God should portion His own desire for the
    work?
The father sends his sons to tend the vineyard,
the first one willingly received the task at first,
but did not at all perform the father's will, as he set forth.
And though the younger one did not accept the charge, he
    finished it

40   in haste. To me he seems the better, but sweeter than both
to the father, is he who takes the charge, and carries out the
    wish.
But having killed the heir, they'd be driven from the vineyard
    and fire would destroy them.
A wedding feast, which the loving father, dear to his excellent
    son,
celebrates rejoicing. I have a part in this.

45   I have a part in this, along with whoever is my friend!
That man remained outside, who placed before the feast
his field, or untrained yoke of oxen, or his wife.

Ἦ ἀγρὸν, ἠὲ βοῶν ζεῦγος νέον, ἠὲ δάμαρτα.
Μηδ' ἐνὶ δαιτυμόνεσσι γαμήλιον εἶδος ἔχουσιν,
Εἵματ' ἔχων ῥυπόωντα, δεθεὶς χεῖράς τε πόδας τε,
50   Νυμφῶνός τε γάμου τε, φίλων τ' ἀπὸ τῆλε πέσοιμι.
Ἡνίκα δ' αἰθομέναις ἁγνῶν δεκὰς ἐν δαΐδεσσι
Παρθένοι ἐγρήσσουσαι, ἀκοιμήτοις φαέεσσι
Νυμφίον ἱμερόεντα Θεὸν δοκέωσιν ἄνακτα,
Ὡς λαμπραὶ γανόωντι ὑπαντήσωσιν ἰόντι,
55   Μή μ' ἐνὶ ταῖς κενεῇσι νόον, καὶ ἄφροσι θείης,
Ἤδη που Χριστοῖο παρεσσομένου μογεούσαις,
Μηδ' ὀλιγοδρανέον δαΐδων σέλας ὄμμασι λεύσσων,
Ὀψὲ φάους ζωῆς ὑγρὸν ποθέοιμι ἔλαιον·
Μηδέ με κληϊσθέντα γάμων ὤσαιτο θύρετρα,   [503]
60   Ἔνθα Λόγος καθαρῇσι πόθου μεγάλοις ὑπὸ δεσμοῖς
Μιγνύμενος κραδίαις θάρσος καὶ κῦδος ὀπάζει.
Ἐκ δὲ γάμων παλίνορσος ἄναξ ἐμὸς εὖτ' ἂν ἐπέλθῃ,
Ἐξαπίνης δοκέουσι, καὶ οὐ δοκέουσιν ἐπιστὰς
Εὕροι μ' ἐν δοκέουσι, καὶ αἰνήσειε φόβοιο
65   Ὡς ἀγαθὸν θεράποντα, καὶ ἤπιον ἀρχομένοισι,
Καὶ σίτοιο δοτῆρα, λόγου στερεοῖο, φέριστον.
Σχιζομένων τ' ἐρίφων καὶ ὀΐων, ἤματι πικρῷ,
Ἀνδρῶν εὐσεβέων τε καὶ οὐχ ὁσίων ἑκάτερθεν,
Στήσαις μή μ' ἐρίφοις ἐναρίθμιον, ἀλλ' ὀΐεσσι
70   Δεξιτερὴν παρὰ χεῖρα, μένοι τ' ἐνὶ χείροσι λαιῇ.
Λύχνος δή τις ἔμοιγε φαεσφόρος ἔκτοθι λάμποι
Λυχνίης καθύπερθε. Καλὸν δέ τι καὶ θεὸν οἷον   [504]
Ἴδμεναι, ὃς πάντεσσιν ἐπίσκοπον ὄμμα τίθησιν.

Let me not be found among the guests wearing their wedding
    dress,
myself in filthy garb, and then bound hands and feet,
50 and so to fall, cut off from friends, the bridal chamber, and
    marriage.
Or when the ten pure virgins, with burning
torches keeping watch, looked out with lights unsleeping
for their ruler, bridegroom, beloved God,
so that, aflame, they went to meet the joyful one approaching,
55 don't put my mind among those dull and senseless ones,
who labor on when Christ is soon to come,
lest I notice all my torches' feeble flame
and seek the flowing oil of the light of life too late.
Let not locked doors restrain me from the wedding,
60 while the mingled Word, within, by using great chains of
    desire,
gives glory and courage to the pure of heart.
And should my king return again from the wedding feast,
to look over the waiting and those not waiting,
me he'd find among the waiting, and would praise me for my
    fear,
65 just like a faithful servant, and find me mild among the ones
    who guard,
and one who gives a reliable account and grain to both in
    fairness.
And when the goats and sheep are split, upon that bitter day,
on either side the holy men and those who are not holy,
may you not set me numbered with the goats, but rather with
    the sheep,
70 upon your right hand, and may your left wait for the worse.
And yet some brilliant lamp shines outside of me,
on high, from the candelabra. Something good and almost
    God
to look on, which puts its overseeing eye on all.

Αἰεὶ δὲ στέργοιμι Θεὸν πλέον, εἴτε τι πικρὸν
75 Εἴτ' ἀγαθὸν παρέχοι· πᾶν γὰρ καλόν. Εἰ δὲ τυπείην
Λῃσταῖς, μεγάλης κατιὼν ἀπὸ Χριστοπόληος,
Μή με λίπῃς χείρεσσιν ὑπ' ἀνδροφόνοισι δαμῆναι.
Εἰ δὲ πνεῦμ' ἐλάσεις ψυχῆς ἄπο, μηκέτ' ἀεργὸν
Εὑρὼν σὺν πλεόνεσσι καταδράμοι ἐχθρὸς ἐμεῖο.
80 Μηδὲ συκῆν ὀλέσειας ἀχρήϊον, ἀλλ' ἔτι καρπὸν
Ἔλπεο, μηδὲ τέμῃς μιν, ἄναξ· κομέων δέ τ' ἐγείρειν.
Δραχμήν τε, πρόβατόν τε, πάϊν τ' ἀπὸ πάντ' ὀλέσαντα
Εὑρὼν, τὴν μὲν ἔραζε, τὸ δ' οὔρεσι, τὸν δ' ὑπὸ ποσσὶν
Οἰκτρὸν ὑποστρέψαντα πατρώϊον ἐς δόμον, ὦ 'ναξ,
85 Αὖθις ἀριθμήσειας ἐν υἱάσι, θρέμμασι, δραχμαῖς.   [505]
Μὴ δ' ἀγαθοῦ βασιλῆος ἐμοῖς παθέεσσιν ἐόντος,
Πρηκτὴρ αὐτὸς ἔοιμι πικρὸς χρήσταις ὁμοδούλοις.
Καί τι χρεῶν κόψαιμι λαθὼν πινυτόφρονι βουλῇ,
Ὥς κεν χρῄζων ποτ' ἐς ὕστερον ἄλκαρ ἔχοιμι!
90 Λάζαρος ἐνθάδ' ἔοιμι, καὶ ὕστερον· ἄλλος ἀγήνωρ
Ἐνθάδε, κεῖθι δ' ἄτιμος ἔχων φλόγας ἀντὶ κόροιο.
Εἴην μὴ μεγάλαυχος, ἐπεὶ κακός εἰμι τελώνης.
Δάκρυσιν οἶκτον ἔχοιμι, Φαρισσαῖοι δὲ πέσοιεν.
Χήρην δ' εἴποτ' ἐμεῖο παρὰ προθύροις μογέουσαν
95 Ἄπρηκτον πέμψαιμι, καὶ εἰ λίθον ἢ ὄφιν αἰνὸν
Ἀντ' ἄρτοιο φίλοιο καὶ ἰχθύος ἡδυβόροιο
Ἐχθρὰ φιλοφρονέων, παλάμης ἀπὸ τῆσδ' ὀρέγοιμι,
Τοίων ἀντιτύχοιμι Θεοῦ πάρα. Εἰ δ' ἀποθήκας   [506]

I love God more and more, regardless if I suffer something
75   painful or something good. For all is good. But should I fall
among the thieves, while departing the great City of Christ[19]
may you not let me be killed by murderous hands.
But if you drive a spirit from my soul, let the enemy
not find me listless, that he may run me down with more.
80   Do not destroy the useless fig, but still have hope
for fruit, and do not cut it off, O king; yet by healing, raise it up.
Finding a drachma, or a sheep, or a son who's wasted all away,
one on the ground, the next in hills, and the other under your
    feet,
the wretched one who turned around, back to his father's
    home, O king,
85   may you count me again among the sons, the sheep, the
    drachma.
And when the gracious king forgives me in my pains,
may I not play the harsh exactor with the debts of fellow slaves.
And let me secretly forgive the debt of those in need, and by
    this cunning plan,
when I'm in need, I might later have support!
90   May I be like Lazarus now, and later, too. The one who
haughty here is later abandoned and has more than enough
    flames.
May I not boast, since I too am an evil tax collector.
I merit mercy by my tears, but the Pharisees would fall.
And should I send away the widow wailing from my gates
95   unrewarded, and if a rock or fearsome snake
rather than good bread and pleasing fish,
as though plotting evil things, I offer from my palm,
I would receive in turn such things from God. But if the
    treasury has

---

[19]Gregory refers to himself leaving "great Christopolis," μεγάλης Χριστοπόληος. The name only occurs here in Greek and may simply refer to his monastic community (often called ουρανοπόλεις in later Byzantine literature).

Τὰς μὲν σφρηγὶς ἔχει, τὰς δ᾽ ἐλπίδες ὦκα θέουσαι,
100 Ἥδε με νὺξ ὀλέσειε σὺν ἀδρανέουσιν ὀνείροις,
Οὐδὲ μὲν οὐδὲ τάλαντον, ὅ μοι Θεὸς ἐγγυάλιξε
Πλειοτέρην ἄλλοισι μετρῶν χάριν, εὔχομ᾽ ἔγωγε
Τοῦτο μένειν παλάμῃσιν ἐν ἡμετέρῃσιν ἀεργὸν,
Ἠὲ μνᾶν φυσικοῖο λόγου, χάριν ἰσονέμητον,
105 Ἀλλ᾽ ἔργον τ᾽ ὀπάσαιμι, κλέους τ᾽ ἐπί τ᾽ ἄντι τύχοιμι·
Μηδὲ δίκην τίσαιμι πικρὴν, καὶ αἶσχος ἔχοιμι.

storerooms, indeed it must have hopes, which quickly vanish,
100 and night would destroy me with vain dreams.
And let not the talent, which God has given me—
that richer grace of meter for others—I pray,
remain without profit in our hands,
but as a *mina* of my native speech let it be a gift fairly measured out.[20]
105 Rather grant that I might create a work, and receive glory in exchange.
May I not pay a harsh penalty, and be put to shame.

[20]The final six lines seem to form a unit that alludes to the parable of the talents (Mt 25.14–30; Lk 19.11–27). They allow Gregory to conclude with a general statement about the aim of his poetry, to bear fruit for his audience. Indeed, he has two talents: the gift of meter in verse, and the gift of his oratory, that is, writing and rhetoric.

Ἄλλα Ποιήματα

I.1.16. Εἰς τὰ θαύματα Ἠλίου τοῦ προφήτου καὶ Ἐλισαίου. (PG 37.477–479)

Τοσαῦτα θαύματ' Ἠλίου τοῦ Θεσβίτου.
Κόραξι πρῶτον ἐτράφη· καὶ δεύτερον
Ἔθρεψε χήραν πλουσίως Σαραφθίαν,
Μικροῖς ἐλαίου καὶ ἀλεύρου λειψάνοις·
5   Ἧς καὶ τὸν υἱὸν ἐκ νεκρῶν φυσήμασιν
Ἤγειρεν. Ὑετόν τ' ἀνέσχεν ἐκ Θεοῦ,
Ἔπειτ' ἀφῆκε. Θυσίαν καταγνίσας   [478]
Πυρὶ ξένῳ τε καὶ ξένοις, εἶτ' ἤρκεσε
Τροφῆς ἄγευστος ἡμέραις ἐν πλείοσι
10 Ἔφλεξεν ἄρδην πεντηκοντάρχας δύω.
Ἰορδάνην διῆλθε μηλωτῇ τεμών·
Πυρὸς δ' ἀνῆλθεν ἅρματι πρὸς οὐρανὸν
Ὁμοῦ δορὰν τε καὶ χάριν Ἐλισσαίῳ
Ἀφῆκεν. Ἄθρει καὶ τὰ τούτου θαύματα·

15 Ἰορδάνην διῆλθε μηλωτῇ τεμών.
Πηγὰς ἔθηκεν ἁλσὶν εὐτέκνους πόλει.
Παῖδας δ' ὑβριστὰς θηρίοις ἀπώλεσεν

Other Biblical Poems

I.1.16. On the miracles of Elijah and Elisha the prophets (PG 37.477–479)[1]

These are the miracles of the prophet Elijah the Tisbite.
First he was fed by a crow (1 Kg 6). Second he himself
fed the Sarephthan woman richly
with small remains of oil and flour (1 Kg 17.14);
5 so he also raised her son from the dead
by breathing on him (1 Kg 17.19–23). He held back the rain by
     God's power,
then he let it come (1 Kg 18.45). He sacrificed the offering
in a strange fire (1 Kg 18.38) and for strangers, since he lived
for many days without tasting food.
10 He entirely burned up two fifty-man armies (2 Kg 1.12).
He went through the Jordan, dividing it with his cloak
     (2 Kg 2.8).
He rose up to heaven on a chariot of fire (2 Kg 2.11).
He left both his cloak and his grace to Elisha (2 Kg 2.12).
Observe, too, the miracles of the latter.
Elisha
15 He went through the Jordan, dividing it with Elijah's cloak
     (2 Kg 2.14).
He blessed the city's fountains with fertility by means of salt
     (2 Kg 2.21).
He killed the haughty children with wild beasts (2 Kg 2.23).

[1]This poem and the next, I.1.17, appear to be out of sequence, later additions to the corpus; they are the only poems on scripture preserved separately, in Groups XV and XX.

Διψῶντι ῥεύματ᾽ ἐξ Ἐδὼμ ἐπήγασε
Στρατῷ· γυναῖκά τε χρέους ἐρρύσατο
20 Πηγαῖς ἐλαίου· τῇ δὲ Σουναμίτιδι
Οὐκ ὄντ᾽ ἔδωκε παῖδα, κ᾽ ἐκ νεκρῶν πάλιν.   [479]
Φθοράν τ᾽ ἐπέσχεν ἐκ πόας, καὶ πλείοσιν
Ἤμυνε λιμὸν ἐνδεεστέρᾳ τροφῇ.
Ναιμᾶν δὲ λέπρας ἐκκαθήρας τὸν Σύρον,
25 Πέμπει Γιεζεῖ τὴν νόσον· εἶτ᾽ ἀξίνην
Ἔπλευσε νώτοις ἐκ βυθῶν Ἰορδάνου·
Σύρων δὲ τοὺς ἕλκοντας ὄψεις ἀμβλύνας
Ἔδωκεν ἐχθροῖς· εἶτα τῷ στρατῷ κόρον
Προεῖτο, λεπρῶν ἔργα. Καὶ νεκρὸς νεκρὸν
30 Ἤγειρεν, ἐγγὺς συντεθέντων ὀστέων.

**I.1.17. Ἐπίγραμμα εἰς τὸ μαρτύριον Ἠλίου
τὸ καλούμενον Χηρεῖον. (PG 37.479–480)**

Αὕτη, ξένε, καὶ Σαρεπτὰ τῆς Σιδωνίας,
Οὗτος δὲ χήρας πύργος, ἢ φιλοξένως   [480]
Θεοῦ προφήτην Ἠλίαν τὸν Θεσβίτην,
Λιμοῦ κακοῦντος τὰς πόλεις, ἐδέξατο·
5 Ἧι καὶ μικρὸν ἦν ἔλαιον ἐν τῷ καψάκῃ,
Καὶ δρὰξ ἀλεύρων ὑδρίᾳ κεκρυμμένος.
Τοῦτο δ᾽ ἀφειδῶς μεταδοῦσα τῷ ξένῳ,
Πηγὴν, τρέφουσαν οἶκον, εὗρε τὴν δόσιν.
Ταύτης τὸν υἱὸν Ἠλίας ζῶντα τρέφων,
10 Θανόντα νεκρῶν ἐξανέστησε ζόφου.
Μήτηρ δὲ, πρὶν κλαίουσα τὴν ἀπαιδίαν,
Ἐγένετο μήτηρ αὖθις ὠδίνων δίχα.

He led streams from Edom to the thirsting army (2 Kg 3.30).
He freed the woman from debts by means of fountains of oil
 (2 Kg 4.4–6).
20 To the Sunammite woman, who was with child
he gave a son, and raised him back again from the dead
  (2 Kg 4.16 and 2 Kg 4.34).
He held off the poison from the grass (2 Kg 4.41), and he saved
many from famine with scanty nourishment (2 Kg 4.43).
He cleansed Naaman the Syrian of leprosy (2 Kg 5.14)
25 And he sent that sickness to Gehazi (2 Kg 5.27). And after
he made axe-heads float from the depths of the Jordan
  (2 Kg 6.6).
He made the enemies, the Syrians, suffer from bleary
eyes (2 Kg 6.18). Then plenty was set before for the army,
the work of lepers (2 Kg 7.16). And, as a corpse he raised a
  corpse
30 when their bodies were laid next to each other (2 Kg 13.21).

I.1.17. Epigram on the martyrion of Elijah, which is called Cherios (PG 37.479–480)

[1 Kg 17]
This, stranger, is indeed Zarephath of Sidon,
and this is the tower of the widow, who hospitably
received Elijah the Tishbite, prophet of God,
while a plague was vexing the cities.
5 She had a little oil in her flask
and one drachma of flour hidden in the water jar.
This she unsparingly gave to her guest.
The well that nourished the household she found as a gift.
Elijah, who nourished her son when he was alive,
10 raised him up from the darkness of the dead.
But the mother, who once bewailed her childlessness,
became a mother again without birth pains.

I.1.28. Χειμὼν ἀπὸ Χριστοῦ κατασταλθείς. (PG 37.506–507)

Ἦν ὅτε Χριστὸς ἴαυεν ἐφ᾽ ὁλκάδος ἔμφυτον ὕπνον,
Τετρήχει δὲ θάλασσα κυδοιμοτόκοισιν ἀήταις.
Δείματί τε πλωτῆρες ἀνίαχον· Ἔγρεο, Σῶτερ,   [507]
Ὀλλυμένοις ἐπάμυνον. Ἄναξ δ᾽ ἐκέλευεν ἀναστὰς
Ἀτρεμέειν ἀνέμους καὶ κύματα, καὶ πέλεν οὕτως.
Θαύματι δ᾽ ἐφράζοντο Θεοῦ φύσιν οἱ παρεόντες.

I.2.25. Κατὰ θυμοῦ. (PG 37.813–851)

Θυμῷ χολοῦμαι τῷ συνοίκῳ δαίμονι,
Οὗτος δίκαιος τῶν χόλων ἐμοὶ μόνος,
Εἰ δεῖ τε καὶ πάσχειν γε τῶν εἰωθότων.
Ἐπεὶ γὰρ ὅρκον τῷ λόγῳ κατείχομεν,
5   Σιγῆς φέροντες καρπὸν ἄξιον λόγου·
Μίαν[1] τιν᾽ ὅρκου ῥίζαν εἰδότες χόλον,
Πολλαῖς σὺν ἄλλαις, αἷς τὸ δεινὸν φύεται,
Τὴν ἀγριωτάτην τε καὶ μελαντάτην·   [814]
Καὶ τὴν, Θεοῦ διδόντος, ἐξαιρήσομεν,
10   Τέμνοντες, ὡς οἷόν τε, τῇ λόγου τομῇ.
Αἰτῶ δὲ[2] πρῶτον, μὴ χολοῦσθαι τῷ λόγῳ.
Οὕτω γάρ ἐστιν ἡ νόσος τῶν ἀσχέτων,
Ὥστ᾽ ἀγριοῦσθαι πολλάκις καὶ ταῖς σκιαῖς,

[1]Πάμπαν PG.
[2]καὶ PG.

I.1.28. The storm calmed by Christ (PG 37.506)[2]

There was a time when Christ slept naturally on the merchant's
    ship,
but the sea rose up with gales that bred waves,
and the seamen cried out in fear: "Rise, Savior,
protect the perishing." The king rose up and commanded
the waves and the winds to rest, and they did so.
Because of this miracle those present spoke of the nature of
    God.

I.2.25. Against Anger (PG 37.813–851)

I rage in my anger, a familiar demon,
which of all angers is the only just one,
if I must still suffer from what is usual.
For since we've suppressed oathtaking by our speech,[3]
5 offering from our silence a fruit worthy of a speech,[4]
knowing for certain that oathtaking has in anger one root
among many others, from which this evil is born,
and it is the most savage and the most foul.
And even this, God willing, we will excise,
10 cutting it out, as much as possible, with the blade of our
    speech.
I first ask that no one grow angry with my speech.
For such is the sickness of the unrestrained
that they often go wild at the sight of mere shadows,

[2]This poem is the most doubtful of the group and, while it appears in two manuscripts of Gregory's poetry, in one of the two it is attributed to Basil (Palla, "Ordinamento e polimetria," 173). Still, see Werhahn, "Dubia und Spuria," 340–341, who, despite some doubts, generally accepts the authenticity of the verse.

[3]Gregory seems to be referring to his poem against oaths, 1.2.24; Oberhaus, *Gegen den Zorn*, 44.

[4]Probably the Lent of 382. Oberhaus, *Gegen den Zorn*, 44.

Αὐτοῖς τε τοῖς σφῶν γνησίοις παραινέταις.

15 Δεῖ δ᾽, ὡς ἔοικε, μή τι μαλθακὸν λέγειν,
Κακοῦ τοσούτου τῷ λόγῳ προκειμένου·
Ἀλλ᾽ ὡς πυρὸς βρέμοντος ἀγρίαν φλόγα,
Πηδῶντος, αἰθύσσοντος ἐντινάγμασι
Πολλοῖς, ἄνω ῥέοντος ἐμψύχῳ φορᾷ,
20 Λάβρως ἀεὶ τὰ πρόσθεν οἰκειουμένου,   [815]
Ὕδωρ, κόνιν πέμποντας εὐνάσαι βίᾳ·
Ἢ θῆρα λόχμης ἐκφανέντα συσκίου,
Φρίσσοντα, πῦρ βλέποντα, ἐξαφρούμενον,
Μάχης ἐρῶντα, καὶ φόνων καὶ πτωμάτων,
25 Λόγχαις, κυνηγοῖς, σφενδόναις καταιχμάσαι
Ἴσως ἂν οὕτω τοῦ πάθους γενοίμεθα
Κρείσσους, Θεοῦ διδόντος, ἤ τι μετρίως
Σχοίημεν. Οὐδὲ τοῦτο τῶν μικρῶν ἐμοί,
Κακοῦ μεγίστου καί τις ἔνδοσις μικρά,
30 Ὡς τοῖς βαρείας ἐκ νόσου στενουμένοις.
Μικροῦ δ᾽ ἄνωθεν τὴν νόσον σκεψώμεθα,
Ἥτις, πόθεν τε καὶ ὅπως φυλακτέα,
Ἀνδρῶν παλαιῶν συλλογὰς σκοπούμενοι,
Ὅσοι διεσκέψαντο πραγμάτων φύσεις.   [816]
35 Εἰσὶν μὲν οἵ λέγουσιν αἵματος ζέσιν,
Τοῦ γειτονοῦντος καρδίᾳ, τὴν ἔκστασιν·
Ὅσοι νέμουσι τὴν νόσον τῷ σώματι,
Ὥσπερ τὰ πολλὰ τῶν παθῶν ἄλλοις τισίν.
Ἄλλοι δ᾽ ὄρεξιν εἶπον ἀντιπλήξεως
40 (Ψυχῇ διδόντες τὴν βλάβην, οὐ σώματι),
Ὀργὴν δὲ τὴν ὁρμῶσαν· εἰ δ᾽ ἔνδον μένει
Λοχῶσα, τοῦτο μνησικακίαν τυγχάνειν
Ὅσοις δ᾽ ἔδοξεν ἡ νόσος τοῦ συνθέτου,
Ζέσιν μὲν εἶπον αἵματος, τὴν δ᾽ αἰτίαν,
45 Ὄρεξιν εἶναι, συντιθέντες καὶ λόγον.
Ταῦθ᾽ ὡς ἔχει μὲν, οὐχὶ νῦν σκοπητέον.
Ἐκεῖνο μέν τοι καὶ λίαν τῶν γνωρίμων,

and also by their own candid counselors.
15   It seems one should not speak delicately here,
when my discourse treats so great an evil.
But just as upon a fire that flares with a fierce flame,
as it leaps out, enkindled by much
shaking, and borne upward by a living force,
20   greedy for whatever is in front of it,
one must cast water and dust to stifle it by force.
Or a beast appearing from a thickly-shaded grove,
heaving, with a gaze of fire, frothing,
yearning for battle and murders and corpses,
25   one must strike down with spears, dogs, and slings;
so perhaps we might thus become greater than
the passion, God granting it, or we might experience it
measuredly. This seems to me no small thing,
even some small relief from the greatest evil,
30   since we are laboring under a heavy sickness.
Let us again consider this sickness:
what it is, where it is from, and how we can guard against it,
considering the opinions of ancient men,
as many as examined the natures of things.
35   For there are those who say that the boiling of the blood
that surrounds the heart, is outrage [*ecstasis*]:
so think those who consider the sickness to be in the body,
just as many things arise from some other passions.
Others (who see the harm in the soul, not in the body)
40   say that rage, when it erupts, is the desire
for revenge. But if the passion remains within
contriving plots, they call this resentment.
But those who consider the sickness of a composite nature
say both that it is a boiling of the blood, but its cause
45   is the desire, and they integrate their account.
But how this stands is not for us to consider now.
For indeed one of the most widely known things

Ὡς νοῦς ἁπάντων ἡγεμών· ὃν σύμμαχον   [817]
Δέδωκεν ἡμῖν κατὰ παθῶν ὁ Δεσπότης.

50   Ὡς οὖν χαλάζης οἱ δόμοι σκεπάσματα,
Θάμνοι δὲ κρημνῶν, καὶ βυθῶν ἐρείσματα,
Τείχη δὲ τοῖς φεύγουσιν ἐκ μάχης τινός·
Οὕτω λογισμὸς πρὸς χόλου παρουσίαν.
Ὅταν καπνίζῃ τὸ φλέγον τὴν σὴν φρένα,
55   Πρὶν πῦρ ἀνάψαι, καὶ ῥιπισθῆναι φλόγα,
Ὅταν ποτ᾽ αἴσθῃ πνεύματος κινουμένου,
Εὐθὺς Θεῷ πλάκηθι, καὶ τόνδ᾽ ἐννοῶν
Ὡς σοῦ προεστῶθ᾽, ὧν τε κινῇ, μάρτυρα,
Αἰδοῖ φόβῳ τε τὴν φορὰν τοῦ πράγματος
60   Ἐπίσχες, ἄχρις ἡ νόσος παρήγορος.
Εὐθὺς βόησον τῶν μαθητῶν ῥήματα·
«Ἐπιστάτα, κλύδων με δεινὸς ἀμφέπει.»
Τίναξον ὕπνον, καὶ σὸν ἐκσώσεις³ στόλον⁴,   [818]
Ἕως λογισμοῦ καὶ φρενῶν ἐπικρατεῖς,
65   Ὧν πρῶτόν ἐστιν ἡ νόσος κατάκλυσις
Ἕως χαλινὸν, ἵππος ὡς δυσήνιος,
Οὔπω δακὼν ὀδοῦσιν ἔρχετ᾽ εὔδρομος,
Πνέων δρόμον τε καὶ φάραγγας, καὶ βάθη,
Θυμῷ σκοτώσας ὀμμάτων ὁδηγίαν.
70   Ῥᾷον γάρ ἐστιν ἀρχόμενον ἄγξαι λόγῳ,
Ἢ πρῶτον ἁρπάσαντα συσφίγγειν⁵ βίᾳ.
Αὐτὸς γὰρ αὑτὸν ἐκκάων οὐχ ἵσταται,
Ἕως λογισμὸν κρημνίσῃ τὸν ἱππότην.
Ἔπειτά μοι, τὸ αἶσχος ἡλίκον, σκόπει,
75   Οἷον τίθησι τὸν κακῶς πεπληγότα.
Τῶν μὲν γὰρ ἄλλων αἱ νόσοι καὶ λάθριοι,

³ἐξώσεις PG.
⁴χόλον PG.
⁵κατασχεῖν PG.

is that the mind is the ruler of all, which the Ruler gave us
as an ally against the passions.
50 Thus, just as our homes are refuges against the hail,
and shrubs protect from cliffs, and bulwarks from pits,
and a wall protects those fleeing from some battle,
so is reasoning against imminent anger.
When the flame sets your heart smoking,
55 before the fire flares up and the flame is fanned,
when you first sense the spirit moving,
immediately embrace God, and consider Him
as appointed witness to that which disturbs you,
and, in your shame and fear, put a stop to the impetus of the
        passion
60 as long as the sickness is responsive.
Call out right away with the words of the disciples:
"Master, the horror of the waves surround me."[5]
Shake off your sleep, and you will save your ship,[6]
until you are master of your reasoning and your thoughts,
65 whose collapse is the first upshot of the sickness.
This happens until the passion, like a restless horse,
biting down on its bit, travels swiftly,
panting on its course over ravines and paths,
in his rage having darkened the wayfinding eyes.
70 For it is easier to constrain by reason someone who's just
        begun
than it is to control by force the one who's been swept away.
For once he is burning he does not stop himself
until he casts down reasoning from its steed.
Therefore consider with me what sort of
75 great shame it creates for the one who is badly struck.
For other sicknesses remain hidden,

---

[5]Cf. Mt 8.24–25; Mk 4.37–38; Lk 8.23–4.
[6]Following Oberhaus's emendation of the PG text, *Gegen den Zorn*, 69.

Ἔρως, φθόνος, λύπη τε καὶ μῖσος κακόν·
Τινῶν δὲ φαίνοντ᾿ οὐδ᾿ ὅλως, ἤ τι βραχὺ,   [819]
Ἀλλ᾿ ἔνδον εἰσὶν αἱ νόσοι κατάσχετοι.
80 Τυχὸν δ᾿ ἂν⁶ ἐκτάκειεν ἐν βάθει φρενὸς,
Πρὶν καὶ γενέσθαι τοῖς ὁρῶσιν ἐκφανεῖς.
Κέρδος δὲ λανθάνουσα καὶ δυσπραγία.
Θυμὸς δ᾿ ὅλον γυμνόν τε καὶ δῆλον κακὸν,
Εἰκὼν προκύπτουσ᾿ οὐχ ἑκόντος σώματος.
85 Εἴ σοί τις ὦπται τῶν ἁλόντων τῷ πάθει,
Οἶδας σαφῶς ὅ φημι, καὶ γράψει λόγος.
Ἔσοπτρον ἐχρῆν ἑστάναι χολουμένοις,
Ὡς ἂν βλέποντες, ἀλλὰ τὴν αὐτῶν ὕβριν
Μικρὸν χαλῷεν, τοῦ πάθους ἐξ ὄψεως,
90 Κατηγόρῳ σιγῶντι κάμπτοντες φρένα.
Ἢ καὶ τόδ᾿ ἔστηκ᾿, αὐτὸς⁷ ὑβριστὴς ὁ σὸς,
Ἐν ᾧ κατόψει σαυτὸν, εἰ σχολὴν ἄγοις.   [820]
Πάθος γὰρ οἷς ἕν, κοινὰ καὶ συμπτώματα.
Ὕφαιμον ὄμμα, καὶ θέσεις διάστροφοι,
95 Τρίχες συώδεις, καὶ γένυς διάβροχος,
Ὠχρὰ παρειὰ, νεκρότητος ἔμφασις·
Ἄλλων ἐρυθρὰ, καὶ μολιβδώδης τινῶν·
Ὅπως ἂν, οἶμαι, καί τινα χρώσας τύχοι
Ὁ βακχιώδης⁸ καὶ κάκιστος ζωγράφος·
100 Αὐχὴν διοιδῶν, ἐγκυλούμεναι φλέβες,
Πνοὴ λόγον κόπτουσα καὶ πυκνουμένη,
Λυσσῶδες ἄσθμα, καὶ φρύαγμ᾿ ἀσχημονοῦν,
Μυκτὴρ πλατύς τε καὶ πνέων ὅλην ὕβριν.
Κρότοι τε χειρῶν, καὶ ποδῶν ἐξάλματα,

---

⁶γὰρ PG.
⁷Ἢ καὶ τόδ᾿ ἔστη καὐτὸς PG.
⁸μανιώδης PG.

such as love, envy, distress, and evil hatred.
Some sicknesses make their appearance not at all, or just a
　　little,
and they can be restrained within.

80　Would that perhaps they would dissipate in the depths of the
　　heart,
before they would become evident to onlookers.
A disgrace that is hidden is actually a gain.
But anger is an utterly naked and obvious evil,
an image emerging from a resistant body.

85　If someone seized by this illness has appeared to you,
you know well what I'm saying, and this account will depict it.
One needs to place a mirror before those who are angry,
so that looking at it, they might at least ease
a bit from their rage, on account of the image of the passion.

90　They rein in their hearts because of the silent accuser.
If you have time to consider, this raging man stands
as an image in which you behold yourself.
For their passion is common and the symptoms the same.
Bloodshot eyes, and twisted limbs,

95　brutish hair, and sweaty cheeks,
pale face like the image of a corpse,
while others are red and others wan as lead.
In such a way I reckon a crazed and wicked painter
would decide to color them.

100　A swelling neck, the veins constricted,
breath blocking the speech and clogging it up,
rabid breathing, and unseemly panting,
flaring nostrils, and breathing all violence,
clapping of hands and stomping of feet,

105 Κύψεις, στροφαὶ, γέλωτες, ἱδρῶτες, κόποι·
Τίνος κοποῦντος; οὐδενὸς, πλὴν δαίμονος.   [821]
Νεύσεις ἄνω τε καὶ κάτω, λόγου δίχα,
Γνάθοι φυσώμεναί τε καὶ ψοφούμεναι,
Ὡς δή τις ἀσκός⁹· παιομένη τε δακτύλοις
110 Ἡ χεὶρ ἀπειλεῖ, καὶ ψόφων προοίμιον.
Καὶ τἀπὶ τούτοις τίς παραστήσει λόγος;
Ὕβρεις¹⁰, ἀραγμὸς, αἰσχρότης, ψευδορκίαι,
Γλώσσης ζεούσης δαψιλῆ ῥαντίσματα,
Οἷον θάλασσα, ἐξαχνιζούσης πέτρας.
115 Λέγει κακὸν τὸ μέν τι, τοῦδ᾽ ὁρμὴν ἔχει,
Τῷδε στενοῦται, καὶ παραυτίκ᾽ ἀγνοεῖ.
Καὶ τοῖς παροῦσιν ἠρεμοῦσι δυσφορεῖ·
Ζητεῖ τὰ πάντα συνδονεῖσθαι τῷ κλόνῳ.
Αἰτεῖ κεραυνοὺς, γίνετ᾽ ἀστραπηφόρος,
120 Αὐτῷ μένοντι δυσχεραίνει τῷ πόλῳ.   [822]
Τὸ μέν τι ποιεῖ τῶν κακῶν, τῷ δ᾽ ἐστιᾷ
Τὸν νοῦν. Φρονεῖ γὰρ, ὡς δράσας ἃ βούλεται.
Κτείνει, διώκει, πυρπολεῖ. Τούτων δὲ τί;
Οὕτω τυφλόν τι καὶ μάταιον ἡ ζέσις!
125 Ἄφωνός ἐστιν, ἀσθενὴς, βοηλάτης,
Ῥήτωρ, Μίλων, τύραννος ἡμῖν ἀθρόως.
Ὁ δυσγενής τε καὶ πένης, τὸν εὐγενῆ,
Τὸν εὐποροῦντα, δυσγενέστατον καλεῖ,
Πένητα· δουλόμορφον, ἡ λώβην¹¹ βροτῶν,
130 Τὸν ἄνθος ὥρας· δυσκλεῆ τὸν εὐκλεᾶ¹²,
Ὁ μηθ᾽ ὅς¹³ ἐστι, μήθ᾽ ὅθεν, λέγειν ἔχων.

---

⁹ἄλως PG.
¹⁰Ὕβρις PG.
¹¹λώβη PG.
¹²εὐκλέα PG.
¹³μηδ᾽ ὅς PG.

105 hunchings, twisting, smirks, sweats, struggles;
But who brings this struggle? None other than a demon.
Nodding up and down, split from reason,
cheeks swelling and whistling,
like a bellows;[7] striking with fingers
110 the hand strikes itself, and is the prelude to strife.
And what account can properly describe what follows?
Violence, clashing, shamefulness, false oaths,
abundant spewings from a raging tongue,
like a sea with rocks covered by foam.
115 One says one bad thing, while someone gets aroused by this
and feels cornered, even as he forgets it right away.
And he takes offense when his surroundings are silent.
He looks for everything to shake along with his own agitation.
He wants thunderbolts, a sky clothed in lightning,
120 and he rages when the sky does not move.
He both commits one evil, and with another he nourishes
his mind. He considers how he can get what he wants.
He slays, he pursues, and he burns. But what comes of this?
Thus is his blazing forth vain and blind!
125 The one who is voiceless, weak, and a lowly cattle driver,
is suddenly an orator, a Milon,[8] and a tyrant.
The one who is base and poor calls the noble
and well-traveled one the basest
and destitute. The one who is the shame of mortals says that
    the one
130 who is the blossom of beauty looks like a slave. The one who
    cannot say
who he is or whence he comes calls the nobleman baseborn.

---

[7]Following the conjecture of Oberhaus, *Gegen den Zorn*, 85.
[8]A greater wrestler of 6 c. BC.

Οὐκ οἶδα κλαυθμὸς, ἢ γέλως τὸ δρώμενον.
Πᾶν ὅπλον ἐστὶ τῷ χόλῳ, καὶ μὴ παρόν.
Πίθηκός ἐστι, καὶ Τυφωεὺς γίγνεται.   [823]
135 Ἀποστρέφει τὴν χεῖρα, κυρτοῖ δακτύλους,
Ζητεῖ λόφον τιν᾽, ἢ τὸν Αἰτναῖον πάγον,
Ὡς σφενδονήσων καὶ μακρὰν βίᾳ χερὸς
Ὁμοῦ βέλος τε καὶ τάφον τῷ δυσμενεῖ.
Τί πῦρ ἐφέξει τὴν ὕβριν, χάλαζα τίς;
140 Ὅταν κενώσῃ τῶν λόγων τὰς σφενδόνας,
Αἱ χεῖρες εὐθὺς, ἀγχέμαχοι προσβολαὶ,
Μάχη βία τε, καὶ κρατεῖ τοῦ δυσμενοῦς.
Ὁ δυστυχέστερός τε καὶ κρατούμενος.
Ἧτταν γὰρ οἶδα τὸ κρατεῖν ἐν χείροσι.
145 Ταῦτ᾽ οὐχὶ δαίμων; καὶ πέρα, πλὴν πτώματος.
Καὶ πτώματ᾽ εἶδον ἔστιν ὧν δονουμένων,
Ὅταν φέρωνται τῇ φορᾷ τοῦ πνεύματος.
Ταῦτ᾽ οὐκ ἀποξένωσις¹⁴ ἐνδήλως Θεοῦ;   [824]
Πῶς δ᾽ οὔ; Θεοῦ γὰρ τὸ πρᾶον καὶ ἥμερον,
150 Οὗ καθυβρίζειν οὐ καλὸν τὴν εἰκόνα,
Μορφὴν ἐπεισάγοντας ἀγνοουμένην.
Οὐδὲν τοσοῦτον ἡμῖν ἡ ἐμπληξία,
Οὔπω τοσοῦτον αἱ νόσοι τῶν σωμάτων.
Ταῦτ᾽ οὐχ ἑκόντων, ἀλλὰ δυστυχῶν πάθη,
155 Εἰ καὶ πονηρὰ, καὶ παροῦσι δάκνομαι

---

¹⁴ἀλλοτρίωσις PG.

I do not know if the one who acts this way is to be pitied or
    mocked.
The angry man has every weapon, even what is not present.
He who is an ape becomes a Typhos.[9]

135 He contorts his hand, he curls his fingers,
he seeks some crest, or the cliff of Etna,
so that faroff he might sling from his violent grasp
a spear together with a tombstone at his enemy.
Why does the flame or the hailstorm not restrain his
    violence?[10]

140 When he ceases the verbal assaults,
immediately his hands engage in fist-fighting blows,
war and violence, and when he overpowers his enemies,
he is in fact more accursed and overpowered himself.
For I know that the one who conquers is in an even worse
    situation.

145 Doesn't the demon do this? And worse, even to his very
    collapse.
And I have seen the collapsing of the agitated ones,
when they are carried by the force of the spirit.[11]
Is this not clearly an exile from God?
How could it not be? For the mild and the gentle is from God,
150 whose image it is not good to deface,
as they do who introduce an appearance that He does not
    recognize.
Insanity is not so bad in our opinion,
nor are illnesses of the body so great a matter.
For these are not sufferings of those who choose them, but
    rather of the unfortunate,
155 even if they are harsh and I am upset by their presence

---

[9]A monster with one-hundred dragon heads.
[10]I.e., the fear of God; cf. Oberhaus, *Gegen den Zorn*, 94.
[11]See John Chrysostom, *On the Incomprehensibility of God*, 5; Is 27.8.

(Τὸ γὰρ παρόν πως τοῖς κακουμένοις πλέον)
Οἴκτου τε μᾶλλον ἢ κατάρας ἄξιον.
Καὶ τῶν κακῶν τὸ δῆλον ἀσφαλέστερον·
Τὸ δ᾽ οὐ δοκοῦσι προσπεσὸν, λυμαίνεται.
160 Μέθη κακὸν μέν· πῶς γὰρ οὔ; τίς δ᾽ ἀντερεῖ;
Καὶ τοῦθ᾽ ἑκόντων· οἱ γὰρ ὧν ἐστ᾽ αἴτιον
Οὐκ ἀγνοοῦντες, ἀλλ᾽ ὅμως ἡττώμενοι,   [825]
Αὐτοὶ προδήλως τοῦ κακοῦ γεννήτορες.
Ἀλλ᾽ οὖν ἐκεῖ μὲν τοῦ κακοῦ τὸ δυσχερὲς,
165 Γέλως, ὃν εἷς ἔπαυσεν ὕπνος αὐτίκα.
Θυμοῦ δ᾽ ὑπερκλύσαντος, εἰ χεῖρον, λέγε,
Τὶ τῶν ἁπάντων οἶδας, ἤ τι φάρμακον;
Ἄλλοις μέν ἐστιν εἰς φρένας πεσὼν Θεός·
Θυμὸς δὲ πρῶτον τῷ Θεῷ φράσσει θύρας,
170 Ἅπαξ ὑπερσχών· ἡ δ᾽ ὑπόμνησις Θεοῦ,
Χεῖρον· συνάπτει καὶ Θεὸν ταῖς ὕβρεσιν.
Αὐτῷ λίθους ποτ᾽ εἶδον, ὦ δεινοῦ πάθους!
Ῥιπτουμένους, κόνιν τε καὶ πικροὺς λόγους.
Τῷ ποῦ, τίσιν¹⁵ τε καὶ ὅπως ἁλωσίμῳ;
175 Νόμοι παρωθοῦντ᾽¹⁶, οὐ διεγνώσθη φίλος,
Ἐχθρὸς, πατὴρ, γυνή τε, συγγενεῖς, ἴσα.
Μιᾶς φορᾶς ἅπαντα, χειμάρρου θ᾽ ἑνός.   [826]
Ἦν καί τις ἐνστῇ, τὸν χόλον μεθείλκυσεν
Εἰς αὐτὸν, ὥσπερ θηρίον ψοφήμασιν,
180 Αὐτός τε χρῄζει συμμάχων ὁ σύμμαχος.
Τούτοις μὲν οὖν μάλιστα κάμπτεσθαι λόγοις·
Οὐ γὰρ δεήσῃ πλειόνων, ἂν εὖ φρονῇς.

---

¹⁵τίσι PG.
¹⁶παρωθοῦνται PG.

(for their presence seems somehow greater to those who are
   afflicted),
but they are worthier of pity than of a curse.[12]
And obvious evils are less dangerous:
while what befalls those who don't expect it is ruinous.
160 Drunkenness is bad. How could it not be? Who would
   contradict me?
And that too is voluntary. These men, not unaware of the
   consequences
still allow themselves to be overcome,
and themselves are clearly the authors of their evil.
But then the baseness of this evil
165 is an occasion for laughter, which one sleep immediately ends.
But tell me, do you know anything that is worse than
an overflowing anger or if there is a cure?
For other evils God can be a cure, when He falls on our
   hearts.
But anger bars the doors to God first of all,
170 once it has taken control. And the mention of God
makes it worse, since one even assaults God with insults.
I once saw rocks cast at Him—O terrible passion!—
and dust and piercing words.
Where and by whom and how is it easily controlled?
175 Laws are rejected, a friend is not distinguished from
an enemy, and father, and wife, relatives, are all the same.
All are subsumed in the one upsurge, the same flood.
And if there were someone who dares resist, he would attract
   anger
against himself, like a wild beast is drawn to noises,
180 and he who tried to be an ally would need his own allies.
But here, above all, we can rest from this argument.
You don't need more, if you think straight.

---

[12]The sequence of vv. 154–157 is wrong; see Oberhaus, *Gegen den Zorn*, 98–99.

Εἰ δ' ἔστ' ἐπῳδῆς χρεία σοι καὶ μείζονος,
Βίους σκόπει μοι τῶν πάλαι καὶ τῶν νέων,
185 Ὅσοι ποτ' ἔσχον ἐκ τρόπου παρρησίαν,
Τίνες μάλιστα προσφιλέστατοι Θεῷ
Τί πρῶτον, ἢ μέγιστον ἐξησκηκότες,
Μωσῆς ἐκεῖνος, Ἀαρὼν, οἱ φίλτατοι,
Δαυὶδ, Σαμουὴλ, εἶτα Πέτρος ὕστερον;
190 Οἱ μέν γε μαστιχθεῖσαν Αἴγυπτον τόσαις
Πληγαῖς ἀσωφρόνιστον εἶχον· ἀλλ' ὅμως
Φειδοῖ προσήγονθ' ὡς τὸ Φαραὼ θράσος,   [827]
Ἕως ἐπεκλύσθησαν ἐκ τῆς ὕβρεως,
Οἷς μὴ τὸ μακρόθυμον ἤνεγκεν σέβας,
195 Ὡς ἂν μάθωσι πάντες αἰδεῖσθαι τόδε.
Κρεῖσσον θρασὺν γὰρ ἢ πρᾷον περιφρονεῖν.
Αἰνῶ Σαμουὴλ, ὅς ποθ' ὕβριν δυσφορῶν,
Ῥήξαντος αὐτῷ τὴν διπλοΐδα τοῦ Σαοὺλ,
Εἶτ' ἀξιωθεὶς, ὥστε[17] συγγνώμην ἔχειν,
200 Ἀφῆκεν εὐθὺς τῷ λόγῳ τὴν αἰτίαν.
Τούτου τί δ' ἂν γένοιτο ἡμερώτερον;
Δαυὶδ ὑπομνήσθητι, καὶ τῶν κρουμάτων,
Ἐξ ὧν πονηροῦ πνεύματος Σαοὺλ ποτε
Ἠλευθέρωσεν· εἶτ' ἀγνώμονος τυχὼν,   [828]
205 Φεύγων, ἀλύων τὸν περὶ ψυχῆς τρέχων[18],
Δοθέντος αὐτῷ τοῦ Σαοὺλ ἐφείσατο
(Καὶ τοῦτο δ' ἴστε), καὶ μόγις σεσωσμένος.
Ἡ διπλοῖς γνώρισμα τῆς ἐξουσίας
Κεκαρμένη, φακός τε τοῦ κράνους κλαπείς.
210 Τί δεῖ λέγειν τὸν υἱὸν ὡς ἠνέσχετο,

---

[17]ὥς γε PG.
[18]δρόμον PG.

But if you need an even greater counsel,
consider with me the lives of the old and the recent,
185 all those who ever had authority through their manner of life:
how did they first and foremost behave,
I mean those most beloved by God
such as Moses and Aaron, the beloved,
David, Samuel, and then later Peter?
190 On the one hand they encountered a senseless Egypt
thrashed by many plagues; but nevertheless
they sought to win them timidly, despite the arrogance of
Pharoah,
until they were overwhelmed by the raging [water];[13]
in the Egyptians patience did not arouse piety,
195 so that all may learn to fear this.
For it is better to consider the case of a rash man than a mild
one.
I praise Samuel, who once suffered an insult
when Saul tore his tunic;
then once he begged him that he should give pardon,
200 he immediately forgave the crime with a word.[14]
What is milder than this?
Remember David, and his harpstrings,
by which Saul once escaped a wretched
spirit.[15] Then when he was ungrateful,
205 David fled, running in flight for his life,
and when Saul was given into his hands, he spared him
(as you well know) and was barely saved himself.[16]
The torn vestment and ornament stolen from his head
were a sign that he was subdued in his power.[17]
210 What is there to say of how David tolerated his own son,

[13]Ex 14.27–28.
[14]1 Sam 15.27.
[15]1 Sam 16.14–23.
[16]1 Sam 23.7–29.
[17]1 Sam 24.5–8, 26.7–12.

Τὸν πατροφόντην, καὶ τύραννον ἀπρεπῆ;
Ὅπου γ' ἐκεῖνον καὶ κλάει τεθνηκότα,
Θρήνοις τε πολλοῖς ἀνακαλεῖται καὶ λόγοις[19],
Τὸν μηνυτήν τε τοῦ πάθους ἀμύνεται,
215   Ὥσπερ λαβών τιν' ἐχθρὸν, οὐκ εὐάγγελον;
Ἡ γὰρ φύσις ἔμπροσθε τῶν ἐγκλημάτων   [829]
Ἔστη, λαβοῦσα τὸν τρόπον συνήγορον·
Ὡς καὶ προσάντης τῷ στρατῷ κατασταθεὶς,
Μικροῦ γενέσθαι τοῦ κράτους ἀλλότριος.
220   Τί δ'; οὐ τὸν ὑβριστὴν Σεμεεὶ ἐκαρτέρει.
Δύσφημον ὄντα τῷ κλέει τῆς εἰσόδου;
Πέτρου δὲ δῆτα τοῦ σοφοῦ τεθαύμακα,
Ὡς μακροθύμως καὶ λίαν νεανικῶς
Ἤνεγκε Παύλου τὴν καλὴν παρρησίαν
225   (Καὶ ταῦτ' ἐν ἄστει τηλικούτῳ καὶ τόσοις
Ἐπαινέταις τε καὶ μαθηταῖς τοῦ λόγου),
Ὡς συντράπεζος οὐ καλῶς ἦν ἔθνεσιν,
Εἰ καὶ τόδ' ᾤετ' ὠφελήσειν τὸν λόγον.
Ἦν γὰρ τὸ κινοῦν καὶ μόνον Θεοῦ φόβος,
230   Ἤ[20] τοῦ λόγου τ' ἔλλαμψις ἐκ κηρύγματος.   [830]
Οὐκ ἂν παρέλθοιμ' οὐδὲ τὸ Στεφάνου καλὸν,
Ὃν οἶδ' ἀπαρχὴν μαρτύρων καὶ θυμάτων.
Λίθοις ἐχώννυτ'· ἀλλ' ὅμως, τοῦ θαύματος!
Μέσος λιθασμοῦ, φθόγγος ἐξηκούετο,

---

[19]ἀνακαλεῖ καὶ γόοις PG.
[20]Ἤ PG.

the parricide and the treacherous tyrant?[18]
How he even mourned him when he died,
calling out with many laments and wailings,
punishing the messenger of the suffering,

215 as though he considered him an enemy, not a messenger of
     good news?[19]
For his nature was such as to take the role of an advocate
before the charges that were raised against Absalom.
So that he even opposed the use of an army,
even until he almost forfeited his own power.[20]

220 What else? Did he not bear the insolence of Shimei,
who insulted the glory of his entrance?[21]
Furthermore I marvel at wise Peter,
how calmly and very bravely
he bore the boldness of Paul

225 (and even in the ancient city and among
so many admirers and disciples of the Gospel),[22]
as claiming that it is not good to share the table with gentiles,
even if he believed it would benefit the word.[23]
For what moved him was the fear of God alone

230 and the illumination of the Word that comes through
     preaching.
But I will not pass over the goodness of Stephen,
whom I know to be the first of martyrs and victims.
He was buried in stones, and, yet, O the wonder!
amid the stoning, his voice was heard,

---

[18] 2 Sam 15.7–12.

[19] Cf. 2 Sam 1.13 and 2 Sam 4.8: Gregory erroneously conflates the notice to the episode of Absalom with the killing of the messenger that happens on the occasion of the death of Saul and Jonathan and that of Ish-Bosheth.

[20] 2 Sam 15.13–14. He seems to refer to the initial attitude of David, who, with the notice of Absalom's revolt, preferred to flee.

[21] 2 Sam 16.5–13.

[22] Antioch.

[23] An error: Paul, in fact, reproved Peter because he avoided the Gentiles for fear of the Jews (Gal 2.11–14).

235 Αὐτός τε συγχώρησιν, ὡς εὐεργέταις,
     Διδοὺς λιθασταῖς, τὸν Θεόν τ' αἰτούμενος.
     Ταῦτ' οὐ προδήλως τῆς Θεοῦ τυπώσεως,
     Καὶ τῶν ἐκείνου καὶ παθῶν καὶ δογμάτων,
     Ὅς ὢν Θεός τε καὶ κεραυνῶν δεσπότης,
240 Ὡς ἀμνὸς ἤγετ' εἰς σφαγὴν ἀφωνίᾳ;
     Ἐμπτυσμάτων τε καὶ ῥαπισμάτων ὅσων
     Ἠνέσχετ'! ἄχρις ὠτίου πεπληγότος
     Τὸ χρηστὸν οἶδε Μάλχος. Οὐκ ἐκραύγασεν
     Ἐνδεικτικόν τι καὶ γέμον παρρησίας   [831]
245 Οὐδ' εἴριξέν τι. Τὸν κακίᾳ τεθλασμένον,
     Ἄκλαστον ἔσχε. Τὴν φρενὸς κουφὴν φλόγα
     Σβέσειν λέγει μὲν, ὡς δὲ χρηστὸς φείδεται,
     Ὡς ἂν κρατήσῃ τῷ πράῳ τὸ συγγενές.
     Τοιαῦτα καὶ τοσαῦτα τοῦ σοῦ Δεσπότου.
250 Οἷς, ἄν τι πάσχῃς²¹, ἀντισηκώσεις τὰ σά,
     Κἂν πάνθ' ὑποστῇς, τὸ πλέον λελείψεται·
     Εἴπερ τὸ πάσχειν κρίνεται πρὸς ἀξίαν.
     Ἀρκεῖ τάδ' ἡμῖν εὐγενῆ παιδεύματα,
     Πλακῶν νόμοι τε καὶ τρόποι τῶν ἐξ ὄρους,
255 Ἢ²² δεῖ τι τούτοις προστεθῆναι καὶ νόθον;
     Καὶ χεῖρον οὐδέν· ὥς τι κἂν τοῖς χείροσι
     Τῶν κρεισσόνων τε καὶ φίλων δρεψώμεθα.
     Ὧν γὰρ κρατεῖν καὶ σφόδρα, οὐ σφόδρ' αἰνετὸν,
     Τούτων κρατεῖσθαι καὶ λίαν, πόσον κακόν!
260 Μεμνήσομαι δὲ καί τινων, καὶ συντόμως.   [832]

---

235 and begging God, he himself gave forgiveness
to the stoners as though they were his benefactors.[24]
Is this not clearly in the imitation of God,
and of his sufferings and teachings,
who although he was God, the one who commands the
thunder,

240 as a lamb was led voicelessly to slaughter?
How much spittle and how many blows
did he endure! Even with his ear cut off
Malchus knew his goodness.[25] He did not cry out
to give evidence of the fullness of his authority,

245 and he did not put up a fight. Though he was bent under by
evil,
he kept himself unbowed. He says that he would snuff out
the light flame of the heart, but in his goodness he spares him,
so that he might overcome his relatives with mildness.[26]
So many and such great characteristics belong to your Master.

250 If you would compare your own sufferings to them,
even if you are placed under all sorts of trials, his will remain
greater,
if you consider the dignity of the one who suffers.
These noble teachings are enough for us,
that is, the laws and the habits of the tablet from the mountain;

255 or is it necessary to add something new to them?
There would be no harm, since we could pluck
from what is worse something greater and dear.[27]
For how great an evil it is to be mastered
by those things which it is not especially praiseworthy to
master!

260 I will mention only some of these briefly:

[24]Acts 7.59–60.
[25]Lk 22.50–51; Jn 18.10.
[26]Compare Is 42.2–3; Mt 12.20.
[27]The pagan exempla that follow.

Παίειν ἔμελλεν ὁ Σταγειρίτης τινά,
Λαβὼν ἐπ' αἰσχροῖς καὶ κακοῖς ἐγκλήμασι·
Θυμοῦ δ' ἐπεισελθόντος ἡνίκ' ἦσθετο,
Ἔστη παλαίων τῷ πάθει, ὡς δυσμενεῖ.
265 Μικρὸν δ' ἐπισχὼν, εἶπεν (ὦ σοφοῦ λόγου!)
«Καινὸν πέπονθας. Προστάτην ἔσχες χόλον·
Εἰ μὴ γὰρ ὀργὴ, κἂν δαρεὶς ἀπηλλάγης.
Νῦν δ' αἰσχρὸν ἦν μοι τῷ κακῷ πλήττειν κακὸν,
Κρατεῖν τε δούλου τοῦ πάθους ἡσσώμενον.»
270 Οὕτως ἐκεῖνος. Τὸν δ' Ἀλέξανδρον λόγος,
Εἰπόντος αὐτῷ Παρμενίωνός ποτε,
Πόλιν τίν' ἐξελόντι τῶν Ἑλληνίδων,
Εἴθ' ὃ δρᾶσαι χρὴ πολλάκις σκοπουμένῳ,
Ὡς, εἴπερ ἦν ἐκεῖνος, οὐκ ἐφείσατο·
275 «Ἀλλ' οὐδ' ἔγωγ' ἂν, εἴπερ ἦν, φάναι, σύγε.
Σοὶ μὲν γάρ ἐστιν ὠμότης, τὸ δὲ πρᾶον   [833]
Ἐμὸν, φυγεῖν τε τὴν πόλιν τοὺς κινδύνους.»
Κἀκεῖνο δ' οἷον, ὡς ἐπαίνων ἄξιον;
Ἐλοιδόρει τις τὸν μέγαν Περικλέα,
280 Πολλοῖς ἐλαύνων καὶ κακοῖς ὀνείδεσι
(Τῶν οὐδὲ τιμίων τις), ἄχρις ἑσπέρας.
Ὁ δ' ἡσυχῇ τὴν ὕβριν, ὡς τιμὴν, φέρων,
Τέλος καμόντα καὶ βαδίζοντ' οἴκαδε
Προὔπεμψε λύχνῳ, τὸν χόλον τ' ἀπέσβεσεν.

the Stagirite[28] wanted to strike someone,
when he received from him shameful and evil reproaches.
But when he perceived the anger entering him,
wrestling with the passion, he stood still, once he grew upset.
265 Holding back a little, he said as in a wise speech:
"You've experienced something new. You've used anger as your
    defender.
For without any wrath you've been set free from the blow.
But now it would be shameful for me to strike an evildoer with
    a second evil,
and that someone so overcome would control another slave of
    the passion."[29]
270 So he said. And then the story of Alexander,
when Parmenion once said to him,
as he considered for a while what he had to do,
when he sacked some city of Greece:
that, if he were Alexander, he would not spare them.
275 Alexander said, "But neither would I if I were you.
For you are cruel, but I am
mild, and the city escapes battle."[30]
And that which follows, how worthy of praise is it?
Someone reviled the great Pericles,
280 harrassing him with many and evil reproaches
(this is someone of no nobility), until the evening.
But he quietly bore the insults, as though they were a prize,
to the end he accompanied him with a lamp, and when he was
    finally
exhausted and arrived home, he thereby quenched his
    bitterness.[31]

[28]That is, Aristotle.
[29]This episode is attributed by Cicero to the Pythagorian Archita of Taranto (*Tuscul.* IV.78), by Seneca to Socrates (*De ira* 1.15.3), and by Diogenes Laertius (3.39) to Plato.
[30]Cf. Plutarch, *Life of Alexander* 29, although Gregory confuses the story, which treats Darius's offer of a marriage alliance.
[31]Plutarch, *Life of Pericles*, 5.2.

285 Ἄλλος δ' ὑβριστὴν, πλουσίαις ἐφ' ὕβρεσι
    Προσθέντ' ἀπειλήν· «Ὡς ὀλοίμην παγκάκως,
    Εἰ μὴ κακὸν κακῶς σε κτείναιμι σθένων.»
    Τούτοις ἀμείβεθ' ὡς φιλανθρώποις λόγοις·
    «Κἀγώ γ' ὀλοίμην, εἴ σε μὴ θείην φίλον.»
290 Κωνστάντιον δὲ (καὶ γὰρ εἰπεῖν ἄξιον,
    Ὡς μὴ τὰ πρόσθεν τυγχάνῃ λόγου μόνα,
    Περιφρονῆτέ θ' ὧνπερ αὐτοὶ μάρτυρες),   [834]
    Φασί ποτ' εἰπεῖν ἄξιον μνήμης λόγον
    Τίς δ' ἦν; ἐκεῖνον τῶν τις ἐν τέλει ποτὲ,
295 Παρώξυν' ἡμῖν, οὐ φέρων τιμωμένους
    Τιμαῖς τοσαύταις (καὶ γὰρ εὐσεβέστατος,
    Εἴ πέρ τις ἄλλος βασιλέων, ὧν ἴσμεν, ἦν)·
    Πολλοῖς δ' ἐπειπὼν καί τινα τοιοῦτον λόγον·
    «Τί τῆς μελίσσης ἐστὶν ἡμερώτερον;
300 Ἀλλ' οὐδ' ἐκείνη τῶν τρυγώντων φείδεται·»
    Ἤκουσε· «Πῶς οὐκ οἶδας, ὦ βέλτιστε σύ,
    Ὡς οὐδ' ἐκείνη κέντρον ἐστὶν ἀσφαλές;
    Παίει μὲν, αὐτὴ δ' εὐθέως ἀπόλλυται.»
    Τοσαῦτ' ἔχεις σὺ τοῦ πάθους τὰ φάρμακα,
305 Πάντων δὲ μεῖζον, ὧν ἔφην, τὴν ἐντολὴν,
    Ἥ μηδὲ τὸν πλήσσοντα ὑβρίζειν ἐᾷ.
    «Οὐ γὰρ φονεύσεις,» τοῖς πάλαι τεταγμένον·
    Σοὶ μηδὲ θυμοῦσθ'²³ ἐστιν ἐντεταγμένον,   [835]
    Μή τοί γε παίειν, μήτε δὴ τολμᾶν φόνον.
310 Τὸ πρῶτον εἴργων, οὐκ ἐᾷ τὸ δεύτερον

²³χολοῦσθαί PG

285 But the other one offered a violent threat,
    including this insult, "I would be utterly ruined,
    if I did not kill you when I could, when you were failing
        terribly."
    Pericles responded with these gracious words:
    "I am also ruined if I don't make you my ally."
290 And they say Constantius (for it is worth mentioning,
    so that my speech does not only contain former events,
    and you contemplate that which you witnessed for
        yourselves),[32]
    once spoke a word worth remembering.
    What was it? One of those in power
295 once provoked him against us,[33] since he could not bear
    that we were esteemed with so many honors (for he was the
        most pious
    of any of the other emperors that we know).
    But this fellow added an additional claim to so many words:
    "What is milder than a bee?
300 But even the bee does not spare the beekeepers."
    Hear the response: "Don't you know, you excellent man,
    how harsh that sting is for the bee?
    Yes, it strikes, but it immediately dies itself."
    You have all of these as remedies for your passion,
305 but greater than all that I've mentioned is the commandment,
    which does not let you attack the one who strikes you.
    "For you shall not kill" was commanded to the ancients.[34]
    What is enjoined on you is not to get angry,
    nor to strike in any case, nor to long for murder.[35]
310 The one who avoids the first, does not allow the second;

[32]Constantius II, who ruled in the western Roman empire from 337 to 361; Gregory expresses a positive judgement on him on another occasion (*Or.* 4.37.5; 16; 21.21) even though the emperor had opposed the anti-Arian party.
[33]He may be referring to his fellow anti-Arians.
[34]Ex 20.13.
[35]Mt 5.21–22.

Τὸ σπέρμ' ἀναιρῶν, τὸν στάχυν κεκώλυκε.
Τὸ μηδ' ὁρᾶν κάκιστα, μοιχείας τομή.
Τὸ μηδ' ὀμνύειν, φάρμακον ψευδορκίας.
Τὸ μηδὲ θυμοῦσθ', ἀσφάλεια πρὸς φόνον.
315 Σκόπει γὰρ οὕτω· θυμὸς ἐκπέμπει λόγον,
Λόγος δὲ πληγὴν, ἡ δὲ πληγὴ τραύματα·
Ἐκ τραυμάτων δὲ τὸν φόνον γινώσκομεν.
Θυμὸς πατὴρ πέφηνε τοῦ πικροῦ φόνου.
Τοῦ μὴ φονεῦσαι τίς ποτ' ἤνεγκε γέρας;
320 Τὸ μηδὲ θυμοῦσθ' ἐστὶ τῶν αἰνουμένων·
Τοῦ μέν γε μισθὸς[24], ἡ φυγὴ τοῦ κινδύνου·
Τούτου δ' ἀμοιβὴ, γῆς μέρος τῆς τιμίας.
Ἄκουε Χριστοῦ, τοῖς πράοις ἃ βούλεται
Ἐν τοῖς μακαρισμοῖς, οἷς ἀπηριθμήσατο,   [836]
325 Τὰ μέτρ' ὁρίζων τῶν ἐκεῖθεν ἐλπίδων.
Τούτου χάριν σοι καὶ νόμους τοίους γράφει.
Παίη παρειάν; πῶς δὲ τὴν ἄλλην ἐᾷς
Ἄκαρπον; εἰ μὲν οὐχ ἑκοῦσ', οὔπω μέγα
Πέπονθε, μεῖζον δ', ἢν θέλης, τὶ λείπεται
330 Καὶ τὴν ἑκοῦσαν πρόσθες, ὡς ἔμμισθος ᾖ.
Χιτῶνα γυμνοῖ; προστίθει καὶ δεύτερον,
Ἔσθημ' ἂν ᾖ σοι καὶ τρίτον, γυμνωσάτω
Τούτων ἔχεις τὸ κέρδος, ἂν πρόῃ Θεῷ.
Ἂν λοιδορώμεθ', εὐλογῶμεν τοὺς κακούς·

---

[24] γ' ὁ μισθὸς PG.

by destroying the seed, he prevents the fruit from maturing.
Thus, not gazing with evil looks is to cut off adultery.[36]
Not to swear at all is the remedy for the false oath.[37]
Not to get angry is the prevention of murder.

315 For consider this: anger leads to a word,
a word to a blow, and a blow to wounds.
And we know that from the wounds follows a murder.
Anger is revealed as the father of a bitter murder.
And who ever received a reward for not murdering?

320 Rather not getting angry at all is worthy of praise.
And its reward is the flight from danger.
Its recompense is inheriting the precious earth.[38]
Listen to Christ, for that which he desired for the mild
in the Beatitudes, where he articulated

325 defining the limits of what can be hoped for in the hereafter.[39]
For this reason he likewise composed the following laws for
you:
Are you struck on the cheek? How do you allow the other
cheek
to be without fruit?[40] If you do it unwillingly, you've hardly
suffered
a great thing, but something greater remains for you, if you
receive it willingly,

330 and you offer the other cheek willingly, so that it might be
rewarded.
Are you stripped of a tunic? Offer a second one, too,[41]
and if you have a third vestment, be stripped of it.
From these you make a profit, if you've offered it to God.
If we are reviled, let us bless the evildoers.[42]

[36] Mt 5.27.
[37] Mt 5.33–37.
[38] Mt 5.5
[39] Mt 5.1–12; Lk 6.20–23.
[40] Mt 5.38–39; Lk 6.29.
[41] Mt 5.40; Lk 6.29.
[42] Mt 5.43–44.

335   Ἄν ἐμπτυώμεθ'²⁵, ἐκ Θεοῦ τιμὴν ἔχειν
      Σπεύδωμεν. Ἐκδιωκόμεθ'; οὔτι καὶ Θεοῦ;
      Τοῦτ' οὐκ ἀφαιρετόν γε τῶν πάντων μόνον.
      Ἄν τις καταρᾶται, σὺ προσεύχου τοῦδ' ὕπερ.
      Δράσειν ἀπειλεῖ; ἀνταπείλει καρτερεῖν.
340   Ἔργων ἔχεται· σὴ πρᾶξις ἀπραξία.²⁶   [837]
      Δύω γὰρ οὕτω τὰ κράτιστα κερδανεῖς·
      Αὐτός τ' ἄριστος τοῦ νόμου φύλαξ ἔσῃ,
      Κἀκεῖνον ἕξεις τῷ πράῳ τῷ σῷ πρᾶον,
      Ἐχθρὸν μαθητὴν, οἷς κρατεῖ νικώμενον.
345   Ὁρᾷς; μάλιστα μέν σε μὴ χολᾶν θέλει·
      Τουτὶ²⁷ γάρ ἐστι καὶ τὸ ἀσφαλέστατον·
      Εἰ δ' οὖν, προλύειν ἑσπέρας τὴν ἔκστασιν
      Δύεσθ' ἐπ' ὀργῇ μὴ δέχου τὸν ἥλιον·
      Εἴτ' οὖν, ὃς ἐκτὸς ὀμμάτων πέμπει βολάς,
350   Εἴτ' οὖν, ὃς ἔνδον τοῖς σοφοῖς αὐγάζεται.
      Δύει γὰρ οὗτος τοῖς πεπληγόσι φρένας,
      Ὡς τοῖς ἀρίστοις καὶ καλοῖς ἐκλάμπεται,
      Πλεῖον τὸ λάμπειν τοῖς βλέπουσιν ἐνδιδούς.
      Τί δ'; οὐ φύσις δέδωκε, φησὶ, τὸν χόλον;
355   Καὶ τὸ κρατεῖν γε τοῦ χόλου. Λόγον δὲ τίς;
      Τίς δ' ὄψιν, ἢ τίς χεῖρας, ἢ ποδῶν βάσιν;   [838]
      Θεὸς τὰ πάντα καὶ φύσις, πλὴν εἰς καλόν.
      Σὲ δ' οὐκ ἐπαινῶ μὴ καλῶς κεχρημένον.
      Οὕτως ἔχει καί τ' ἄλλα τῆς ψυχῆς πάθη.
360   Δωρήματ' ἐστὶν ἐκ Θεοῦ, κινούμενα
      Λόγου ποδηγίᾳ τε καὶ στρατηγίᾳ.
      Ζήλου μὲν ὅπλον θυμὸς ἐμμέτρως πνέων·

---

²⁵ἐκπτυώμεθ' PG.
²⁶ἡ εὐπραξία PG.
²⁷Τοῦτο PG.

335 If we are spit on, let us yearn to have our honor
  from God. Are we persecuted? But does that not come from
    God?
  This alone of all things cannot be taken from us.
  If someone curses you, pray for him.
  Does he threaten to do something? Threaten to endure in
    return.
340 If he really acts: let your act be not acting.
  For thus you gain the two greatest profits.
  You will yourself be the best observer of the law,
  and you will make the other one mild by your mildness,
  making an enemy into a disciple, overcome in those matters
    where he wanted to control.
345 Don't you see? Christ desires most of all that you not get angry:
  for this is the most secure approach;
  but if you are still overcome, drive out the disturbance
  before evening, and do not allow the sun to set on your
    anger:[43]
  either the sun outside of our eyes, which sends forth its rays,
350 or the one that shines within the wise.
  For this sun sets on the heart suffering attacks,
  even as it shines out for the good and the virtuous,
  permitting them to look on its greater shining.
  But what? Did not nature, one asks, give us anger?
355 But also the controlling of anger. Who has given us reasoning?
  Who gives sight, or hands, or the stability of feet?
  God and nature gave them all, but only for a good end.
  I do not praise you for not using them well.
  All the other passions of the soul are like this.
360 They are gifts from God, being moved
  by the guidance and rule of reason [the Logos].
  For an anger that seethes according to measure is a weapon
    against zeal,

[43]Eph 4.26.

Πόθου δὲ χωρὶς οὐχ ἁλώσιμος Θεός.
Λογισμὸν οἶδα τῶν καλῶν διδάσκαλον.
365 Εἰ δ' εἰς τὰ χείρω ταῦτα τὴν ῥοπὴν ἔχοι.
Ὁ μὲν χέων ὕβριν τε καὶ μοχθηρίαν,
Ὁ δ' εἰς κακίστας ἡδονὰς οἰστρηλατῶν,
Ὁ δ' οὐ κατάγχων ταῦτα, καὶ πλοκὰς στρέφων,
Οὕτω τὰ καλὰ γίγνεται τοῦ φθορέως.
370 Θεοῦ δὲ δῶρον οὐ καλὸν κακῷ φέρειν²⁸.
Θεὸν δ' ἀκούων ἐν Γραφαῖς χολούμενον,
Ἢ πάρδαλίν τιν', ἢ παροιστρῶσαν πόθῳ   [839]
Ἄρκτον, ζέοντα ἐκ μέθης καὶ κραιπάλης,
Ἢ καὶ μάχαιραν τοῖς κακοῖς στιλβουμένην.
375 Μὴ τοῦτο ποιοῦ τοῦ πάθους παρήγορον
Ὧι προσπλακείς, ζητεῖς γὰρ οὐ λύσιν κακοῦ
Καλῶς ἄκουε, μὴ κακῶς, τοῦ πράγματος.
Πάσχει γὰρ οὐδὲν ὧν ἐγὼ πάσχω Θεός.
Μή τις τοῦτ' εἴπῃ· καὶ γὰρ οὐδ' ἐξίσταται
380 Αὐτός ποθ' αὑτοῦ. Ταῦτα γὰρ τοῦ συνθέτου,
Καὶ τῶν μάχεσθαι ἠργμένων ἐκ πλείονος.
Ὁ δ' ἔστι, τοῦτ' εὔδηλον, ἄτρεπτος φύσις.
Πῶς οὖν τυποῦται ταῦτα; τῆς τροπῆς νόμοις.
Πῶς; δειματῶσαι τῶν ἁπλουστέρων φρένας,
385 Ὥσπερ τὰ πολλὰ τῶν λόγῳ δηλουμένων.
Ἀντιστροφὴν νόει δὲ²⁹, καὶ τὸ πᾶν ἔχεις.   [840]
Ἐπεὶ γὰρ αὐτοὶ πλήσσομεν χολούμενοι,
Χολᾶν τὸ πλῆσσον τοὺς κακοὺς ἐγράψαμεν,

²⁸φύρειν PG.
²⁹γὰρ PG.

and without desire God is not attainable,
and I know that reasoning is the teacher of good things.
365 But if they bring an impetus to what is worse,
the one [anger] pouring out violence and depravity,
while the other [desire] driving mad in deceiving pleasures
and the last [reasoning] does not rein these in, but even weaves
in deception,
so that what is good becomes corrupt.
370 It is no good thing to lead the gift of God to evil.
You hear of God getting angry in the Scriptures,
like a leopard or a bear disturbed
by yearning,[44] seething from drink or gluttony,[45]
or a sword glittering for evildoers.[46]
375 Do not make this a justification for the passion,
and thereby attaching yourself to it, you seek an excuse for
your evil;
listen well, not poorly, to the fact of the matter.
For God suffers nothing like I suffer.
Let no one say this. For indeed
380 He is never separated from who He is. For this obtains only for
a composite being,
and for those who began long ago to struggle for that claim.[47]
Who He is—and this is very clear—is an unchanging nature.
Then how is it that such things are expressed of Him? By the
rules of a way of speaking.
How? To frighten the souls of the very simple,
385 Just like many things presented by Scripture.
But consider the turn of phrase and you understand it all.
For since when we get angry we punish,
we wrote that the smiting of evildoers is His getting angry,

[44]Hos 13.7–8.
[45]Ps 78.65.
[46]Ps 7.13.
[47]I.e., that Christ is composite; Oberhaus, *Gegen den Zorn*, 154, attributes this
position to the Apollinarians.

Ὡς ὄψιν, ὦτα, χεῖρας ἐξευρήκαμεν,
390 Οἷς χρώμεθ᾽ αὐτοὶ, τῷ Θεῷ δεδωκότες,
Ἐπάν τι τούτων, ὡς δοκεῖ, ἐργάζεται.
Ἔπειτ᾽ ἀκούεις τοὺς κακοὺς, οὐ τοὺς καλοὺς,
Ὀργῇ Θεοῦ πάσχειν τι καὶ δίκης νόμοις·
Ὁ σὸς δὲ θυμὸς οὐ μέτροις ὁρίζεται.
395 Πάντας δ᾽ ἴσους τίθησι. Μὴ τοίνυν λέγε
Ὡς ἐκ Θεοῦ σοι, καὶ Θεοῦ τὸ σὸν πάθος.
Ἢ καὶ φρονεῖς σύ γ᾽ ὡς Θεὸν μιμούμενος;
Ζήλωσον, ἀλλὰ τὴν νόσον γ᾽ αὔραις δίδου.
Εἴ που δ᾽ ἀνέγνως εὐσεβῶν ἀνδρῶν χόλους,
400 Πάντας δικαίους εὗρες. Οἶμαι δ᾽ οὐ χόλους,   [841]
Κακοῖς δὲ πληγὰς ἐνδίκως κινουμένας.
Οὔπω γὰρ ἦν ἐκείνοις ἡ πληγὴ κακόν·
Πληγαὶ δ᾽ ἐκείνοις σφόδρα συμφορώτατον,
Χρῄζουσι πολλῆς τοῦ βίου καθάρσεως,
405 Ῥάμνου σίδηρον ὀξὺν ἐκκαλουμένης,
Νόμου τε πρόσθεν, καὶ πρὶν ἰσχύσαι νόμον
Οὔπω τελείως τοῖς τότ᾽ ἐρριζωμένον.
Οὕτω μὲν οὖν σὺ τὴν νόσον κατασβέσεις,
Τούτοις σεαυτὸν³⁰ ἐκμαλάσσων τοῖς λόγοις,
410 Ὡς οἱ κατεπάδοντες ἀσπίδων γένους
Οἴσεις δὲ δὴ πῶς; τοῦτο γάρ σοι δεύτερον.
Μή πως³¹ πυρὸς πῦρ ἐκκάῃ χόλου χόλος·
Ἴσον γάρ ἐστιν αὐτὸν ἄρξασθαι κακοῦ,
Ἄλλῳ τε κινηθέντι συμπαθεῖν κακῶς.   [842]
415 Πρῶτον μὲν αὖθις³² πρὸς Θεὸν κατατρέχων,

---

³⁰τε σαυτὸν PG.
³¹που PG.
³²εὐθὺς PG.

and so we have imagined Him with eyes, ears, hands,
390 giving to God what we ourselves possess,
when it seems to us that by these members something is
accomplished.
But then you hear that the evil, and not the good,
suffer the anger of God also according to the rules of justice:
but your anger is bound by no measure.
395 Rather, it treats everyone the same. Don't say then that
your passion comes from God, and is fitting for God.
But do you still imagine that you are imitating God?
Look to do so, but cast your sickness to the winds.
But if you read that there are angry men among the pious,
400 you find that all of them are just. Yet I do not consider them
angry,
but rather rightfully moved to punish evil.
For the wicked the punishment was not a bad thing:
but rather the blows were most profitable for them,
since they had need of a great purification of their life,
405 as when the underbrush demands a knife;
the law did not yet exist, and this law was not strong
since it was not yet perfectly rooted in the men of that time.
Thus you will fully quench your sickness,
by soothing yourself with such accounts,
410 like those who enchant all types of serpents with songs.
And how should you endure this? This is the second thing to
consider.
Let not anger be ignited by anger just as fire is by fire.
For it is the same thing to start one evil
and to be viciously swept up by another that's been incited.
415 First of all run yet again to God,

Αἰτῶν τε τὴν χάλαζαν ἐκτρέψαι³³ κακοῖς³⁴,
Ἡμῶν δὲ φείδεσθ' οὐδὲν ἠδικηκότων·
Σταυρῷ τε σημειούμενος παραυτίκα,
Ὅν πάντα φρίσσει καὶ τρέμει, ᾧ πάντοτε
420 Πρὸς ταῦτα³⁵ οἶδα προστάτῃ κεχρημένος·
Ἔπειτα σαυτὸν εὐτρεπίζων πρὸς πάλην
Τοῦ τὸν χόλον κινοῦντος οὐ χολουμένον³⁶,
Ὡς ἄν κρατήσῃς τοῦ πάθους ὡπλισμένος.
Τὸ μὲν γὰρ οὐχ ἕτοιμον οὐδ' ἀνθίσταται·
425 Ὅ δ' ηὐτρέπισται, τοῦτο καὶ νικᾶν σθένει.
Τὸ δὲ κρατεῖν τί; τὸ κρατούμενον φέρειν
Τρίτον σεαυτὸν μὴ μεγίστων ἀξιῶν,
Εἰδὼς ὅθεν³⁷ προῆλθες, ἢ οἶ³⁸ καταστρέφεις·   [843]
Ὡς μὴ ταράσσῃ τὸ παρ' ἀξίαν τὸ πνέον³⁹.
430 Τὸ γὰρ ταπεινὸν καὶ φέρει νικώμενον.
Οὐ κάμπτεται δὲ τὸ σφόδρ' ἐξωγκωμένον.
Σποδὸν δὲ, καὶ γῆν, καὶ σκιὰν καλουμένους
Αὐτοὺς ὑφ' αὑτῶν οἶδα τοὺς Θεῷ φίλους,
Ὡς ἄν σε⁴⁰ συστέλλωσι τῆς ἐπάρσεως.
435 Σὺ δ', ὡς ἄριστος, τὰς ὕβρεις ἀπαξιοῖς;
Μὴ καὶ δίκας ὄφλῃς γε τοῦ φρονήματος.
Πῶς δ' ἄν παθῶν ἔργῳ τι τῶν οὐχ ἡδέων
Στέρξαις, ὃς οὐδὲ ῥήματ' εὐπετῶς φέρεις;
Τέταρτον, εἰδὼς οὐδὲν ὄντα τὸν βίον,
440 Ἀλλ' οὐδὲ κριτὰς ἀπλανεῖς τῶν πραγμάτων
Ἅπαντας ὄντας τῶν καλῶν ἢ μὴ καλῶν·
Στροβούμενον δὲ καὶ περιπλανώμενον

---

³³ἐκτρίψαι PG.
³⁴κακῶς PG.
³⁵πάντας PG.
³⁶χολουμένου PG.
³⁷ὅπως PG.
³⁸οἶ *om.* PG.
³⁹πνέειν PG.
⁴⁰τι PG.

begging Him to wipe out evildoers with His hail,
and to spare us who have done nothing wrong.
Immediately sign yourself with the cross,
before which all fear and tremble, and in which I know
420 that I am always benefited as a defense before all things.
Then prepare yourself for the struggle
with the one who causes anger, while you are not angry,
so that, armed in this way, you might control this passion.
For the one who is not prepared cannot withstand it:
425 but the well prepared can also conquer this by his strength.
But what is it to conquer? To allow yourself to be conquered.
Third, do not reckon yourself among the best,
knowing how you came into the world and how you will be
     destroyed:
so you will not be disturbed to aspire beyond what you
     deserve.
430 For the humble allows himself to be defeated,
but the one who is very puffed up will not bow down.
And I know that those who are friends of God
call themselves ash, and earth, and darkness,
so that they might rein themselves in from pride.
435 But do you disdain rebuke, as though you were the noblest?
May you not become guilty of the charge of arrogance.
For how can you acquiesce to a suffering that is truly
     unpleasant
when you do not even take words lightly?
Fourth, know that life is nothing
440 and also that not everyone is an honest judge of deeds
that are good and not good.
Most of us, my good friend, are confused

Τὸ πλεῖον ἡμῶν, ὦ 'γάθ', ἐν τοῖς πλείοσι.   [844]
Ἃ μὲν γὰρ ἡμῖν αἰσχρὰ οὐχὶ καὶ Λόγῳ·
445 Ἃ δ' οὐκ ἔμοιγε, ταῦτα τῷ Λόγῳ τυχόν.
Ἔν ἐστι πάντως αἰσχρὸν, ἡ μοχθηρία,
Τὸ δοξάριον δὲ τοῦτο, καὶ τὸ εὔπορον,
Ἤ τ' εὐγένεια, παιδίων ἀθύρματα.
Ὥσθ' οἷς μὲν ἄχθομ', ἐντρυφᾷν ἐχρῆν ἴσως·
450 Οἷς δ' ὀφρυοῦμαι, καὶ ταπεινοῦσθαι πλέον,
Ἤ νῦν ἐπαίρομ' οὐ καλῶς φυσώμενος.
Πέμπτον, λογισμῷ μείζονι χρησώμεθα.
Ὡς εἰ μὲν οὐκ ἀληθὲς οὐδὲν, ὧν λέγει,
Ὁ τῷ χόλῳ ζέων τε καὶ τυφλούμενος,
455 Οὐδὲν πρὸς ἡμᾶς· εἰ δ' ἀληθεύει λέγων,
Ἐμαυτὸν ἠδίκηκα, καὶ τί μέμψομαι
Τὸν ἐκλαλήσανθ' ἃ πρὶν ἦν κεκρυμμένα;
Χόλος φυλάσσειν πίστιν οὐκ ἐπίσταται   [845]
Ὅς γὰρ καθίστατ' οὐκ⁴¹ ἀληθὴς⁴² πολλάκις,
460 Πῶς ἂν κατάσχοι μοι χόλος μυστήριον;
Ἔπειτ' ἐκεῖνο σωφρονήσεις ἐννοῶν,
Ὡς εἰ μὲν οὐδέν ἐστιν ἡ ζέσις κακὸν,
Οὐδ' ἐγκαλεῖν δίκαιον· εἰ δ' ἔστι κακὸν,
Ὡς ἔστι, καί σοι φαίνεται, μὴ αἰσχρὸν ᾖ
465 Πάσχειν, ἃ τοῦ πάσχοντος εἶ κατήγορος,
Καὶ μὴ τὸν ἐχθρὸν λαμβάνειν παραινέτην;
Εἶτ' εἰ μὲν ἔστι πρόσθεν οὐκ αἰνούμενος
Οὗτος, ὁ νῦν ζέων τε καὶ πνέων θράσος,
Καὶ νῦν προδήλως ἀντὶ σοῦ μεμφθήσεται.
470 Εἰ δ' ἂν καλῶν τις, οὐ σὺ δόξεις σωφρονεῖν.
Πρὸς γὰρ τὸ κρεῖσσον ἡ ῥοπὴ τῶν πλειόνων.
Ἀλλ' εὖ πέπονθε; πλεῖον ἐγκληθήσεται.

⁴¹οὐδ' PG.
⁴²ἀληθὲς PG.

and much deceived, in many matters.
For what is shameful for us is not so for the Logos.
445 And that which is not for me, just might be for the Logos.
One thing is totally shameful, that is badness,
while a bit of honor and wealth
and good birth are the trifles of children.
So I perhaps might have to revel in what pains me;
450 but in that fact I would take pride, since it is better to be
　　　humble,
rather than that I be swept up wrongly in arrogance.
Fifth, let us employ a better reasoning.
For if there is nothing true in what one
who is boiling with anger and is blinded says,
455 they mean nothing to us. But if he speaks the truth,
I have harmed myself, and why should I blame
the one who expresses what was previously hidden?
Anger does not know how to preserve faithfulness,
for how could the anger that often offers what is not true
460 ever keep a secret for me?
Further you would be wise to consider
that if the raging is not evil
it is not right to condemn it. But if it is evil,
as it is indeed, and as it seems to you, is it not shameful to
　　　suffer
465 that which you accuse in the one who suffers it,
and not rather to take your enemy as a goad for yourself?
And if he who was not formerly esteemed
now rages and pants arrogance,
even now he clearly will be blamed instead of you.
470 But if he is a virtuous man, you will not seem wise [if you grow
　　　angry].
For the inclination of the majority is in favor of the better man.
But did he benefit from you? Even more will he be condemned.

Ἀλλ' ἠδίκηκέ⁴³ σ'; αὐτὸν οὐ δράσεις κακῶς.   [846]
Ἀλλὰ σχεθήσετ'; ἂν δὲ πλεῖον ἐκμανῇ.

475 Ἀλλὰ προήρξατ'; ἀλλὰ κλασθήτω τάχος
Τῷ σῷ λόγῳ τε καὶ τρόπῳ περιτραπείς,
Ὥσπερ τι κῦμα λυθὲν ἐν χέρσῳ τάχος,
Ἢ καὶ ζάλη τις οὐκ ἔχουσ' ἀντίστασιν.
Ὕβρις τάδ' ἐστίν; ὕβρις, ἢν συνεκπέσῃς.

480 Ἢ καὶ νοσοῦσιν ἀντιλοιδορήσομεν;
Τῶν δαιμονώντων οὐ φέρεις τὴν ἔκστασιν⁴⁴;
Τούτων λέγω δὴ τῶν ὑλακτούντων βίᾳ.
Τοὺς ἔκφρονας δὲ καὶ δεινῶς μεμηνότας;
Ἄν εὖ φρονῇς γε· τοὺς μεθυπλῆγας δ' ἔτι,

485 Ὧν τὴν φρόνησιν ἡ μέθη κατέκλυσε.
Τί δ' εἰ κύων σοι προσδράμοι λύσσης γέμων;
Τί δ' ἂν κάμηλος φυσικῆς ἐξ ὕβρεως
Βροντῶσα λαιμῷ, καὐχέν' ἐκτείνουσά σοι,   [847]
Στήσῃ παλαίων; ἢ τὸ φεύγειν σώφρονος;

490 Τί δ' εἴ σε πόρνη τοῖς ἑαυτῆς αἴσχεσι
Βάλλοι; σύνηθές σφόδρα⁴⁵ γὰρ πόρναις τόδε,
Αἷς ἐστι δεινὸν αἶσχος, αἶσχος εἰδέναι,
Τέχνην ἐχούσαις μηδὲν αἰσχύνεσθ' ὅλως.
Ὁ δ' ἐκ Σινώπης προσιὼν ταῖς ἐκ στέγους,

495 Ὕβριζε ταύτας, ὡς λόγος· τί μνώμενος;
Φέρειν τὰς ὕβρεις εὐκόλως ταῖς ὕβρεσι.
Ταῦτ' ἐννοῶν σὺ τὰς ὕβρεις ἀτιμάσεις.
Εἴπω τι τεχνικὸν μὲν⁴⁶, οὐ μὴν ἄξιον
Τοῖς τὸ πρᾶον τιμῶσιν· ἀλλ' ὅμως ἐρῶ.

500 Σβεστήριον γάρ ἐστι τῆς ἀηδίας.
Πύκτας ποτ' εἶδες; ὡς τὸ πρῶτον ἡ στάσις

---

⁴³ἠδίκησέ PG.
⁴⁴ἔνστασιν PG.
⁴⁵ἐστι PG.
⁴⁶τι καὶ τεχνικὸν PG.

Or did he do you wrong? You will not treat him badly in
    return.
But will you remain calm? Perhaps he would rage all the more.
475 But did he act first? Fine, but let him be quickly deflected
by your words and behavior to convert,
like a wave that quickly dissolves upon the shore,
or like a storm that meets no opposition.
Is this violence? Violence, yes, if you are caught up in it.
480 Or perhaps we injure in turn those who are sick?
Do you not endure the assaults of the demon-possessed?
I speak of those who bark out involuntarily,
or the insane or those terribly out of their minds.
Rather you would wisely consider them much like the
    inebriated,
485 whose sense drinking has dissolved.
And what if a dog full of rage charges at you?
What if a camel, from its natural insolence,
thundered with its gullet, extending its neck at you,
would you stand there to fight? Or wisely flee?
490 But what if a harlot would attack you with
her disgraceful deeds? Indeed, this is the way of harlots,
for whom it is a terrible shame to know shame in the first
    place,
for their skill is not to experience shame at all.
There was a man from Sinope, who, as he approached those
    from the brothel,
495 rebuked them, so they say. Why do I recall this?
Bearing insults is done more easily by means of insults.
Thinking about this you will disregard these insults.
I want also to speak of a technique, not worthy of those
who esteem mildness, but I will say it anyhow.
500 For it can quench disgust.
Have you seen boxers? How first their battle

Τούτοις ἀγώνισμ᾽ ἐστίν, ὑψηλὴν λαβεῖν;
Οὐ γὰρ μικρόν τι τῷ κρατεῖν συνεισφέρει.   [848]
Οὕτω θέλησον αὐτὸς ἦν λῷον λαβεῖν.
505 Ἡ δ᾽ ἔστι τὸν λυσσῶντα βάλλειν παιγνίοις.
Γέλως μέγιστον ὅπλον εἰς ὀργῆς μάχην.
Ὡς οἱ κενὴν⁴⁷ πέμποντες ἀθληταῖς χέρα
Ὁρμήματι σφοδρῷ τε καὶ θυμουμένῳ⁴⁸
Κάμνουσι πλεῖον τῶν πονούντων σωμάτων
510 (Κράτημά τ᾽ οὐκ ἔντεχνον ἰσχύος κλάσις)·
Οὕτως ὃς ὑβρίζει μὴ χολούμενόν τινα,
Ἀλλ᾽ ἐκγελῶντα τὴν μάχην, ἀλγεῖ πλέον.
Τὸ δ᾽ ἀντιπῖπτον καί τιν᾽ ἡδονὴν φέρει.
Πλείων γὰρ ὕλη τῷ χόλῳ καθίσταται,
515 Λίαν γλυκεῖ τε καὶ ἀπλήστῳ πράγματι.
Ἐκεῖνό σοι γένοιτο τῆς βουλῆς τέλος.
Τί τὸ πρᾶον μάλιστα τῶν ὄντων; Θεός.
Τίς δ᾽ ἡ χολώδης φύσις; ὁ βροτοκτόνος.   [849]
Ὀργήν γέ τοι γίνωσκε καὶ καλούμενον,
520 Πρὸς αἷς καλεῖται κλήσεσιν⁴⁹ πονηρίας.
Τούτων ἑλοῦ τιν᾽ ἣν θέλης μοῖραν σύγε·
Ἄμφω γὰρ οὐκ ἔνεστι. Καὶ τοῦτο σκόπει·
Τίς μὲν γελᾶται, τίς δὲ τῶν αἰνουμένων;
Μικρὸν γὰρ οὐδὲ τοῦτο τοῖς σκοπουμένοις.
525 Τί⁵⁰ λοιπόν, ὁρκίζω σε τὸν κακὸν⁵¹ φίλον,
Τὸν δυσμενῆ συνήγορον καὶ προστάτην,
Οἰδοῦντα καὶ διδόντα⁵² ταῖς ᾅδου πύλαις,
Εἶξαι Θεῷ τε καὶ Λόγῳ τὸ σήμερον,
Θυμέ, ζέσις, πλήρωμα τοῦ βροτοκτόνου,

---

⁴⁷κεινὴν PG.
⁴⁸μεμηνότι PG.
⁴⁹κλήσεσι PG.
⁵⁰Τὸ PG.
⁵¹τῶν κακῶν PG.
⁵²διδοῦντα PG.

is for position, to take the higher part?
This contributes no small part to the conquest.
So you yourself should wish to take the better position,
505 which is to fight the raging one with jokes.
For laughter is the greatest weapon against an assault of rage.
As those who cast their hands in vain on wrestlers
grow more weary from the great rush and the anger
than they do from the toiling of the bodies
510 (for the dextrous grasp means no loss of strength),
so he suffers more who does violence to whoever
does not get angry, but rather laughs at the battle.
Indeed, the act of opposing brings a sort of pleasure.
For it supplies more material to the anger,
515 which is a very mindless and insatiable thing.
Let this be the end of our counsel.
What then is the mildest of all beings? God.
And who has the irascible nature? The homicide.
In any case know that this is also called rage,
520 in addition to other names of wretchedness by which it's
    named.
But yours is to choose which lot you want.
For both are not possible. And consider this:
who is mocked and who is praised?
For this is no small thing for those who consider it.
525 Otherwise I vow that you, O wicked friend,
the wretched supporter and protecter,
who make men swell up and give them to the gates of Hades,
to submit this day to God and to the Word,
O Anger, you boiling, fullness of homicide,

530 Αἶσχος προσώπων⁵³ ἐμφανὲς, φρενῶν ζάλη,
    Μέθη μύωψ, κρημνιστὰ, ταρταρηφόρε.   [850]
    Ὦ πνευμάτων λεγεών, κακὸν σύνθετον,
    Δεσμοὺς διασπῶν καὶ πέδας σὺν ἄμμασιν,
    Χριστός σε βούλεθ᾽, ὃν τὸ πᾶν τόδ᾽ οὐ φέρει,
535 Αὐτὸς φέρει δ᾽ οἴαξιν ἀπταίστως τὸ πᾶν,
    Νωμῶν βροτῶν τε καὶ τῶν ἀγγέλων βίον,
    Ὃς καὶ πονηρῶν πνευμάτων λύσιν φέρει
    Παθῶν τε, τοῖς καλοῦσιν αὐτὸν ἐκτενῶς,
    Οὗτός σε βούλετ᾽ ἔνθεν ὡς τάχος φυγεῖν·
540 Τῶν σῶν συῶν πλήρωσον εἰσελθὼν βάθη·
    Δέξονθ᾽ ἑτοίμως εἰς βυθοὺς⁵⁴ πεσούμενον.
    Ἡμῶν δ᾽ ἀπόσχου τῶν Θεῷ μεμηλότων.
    Καὶ ταῦτα σιγῆς· οἱ δὲ λύσαντες λόγον,
    Εἰ μέν τοι τούτων ἄξιον φθέγγοισθ᾽ ἔπος,   [851]
545 Φθέγξασθε κἀμοί· εἰ δὲ σιγῆς, οὐκ ἐμοί.
    Καὶ ὦτα δήσω τοῖς λόγοις, ὥσπερ λόγον.

I.1.33. Εὐχαριστήριον. (*dubium* PG 37.514)

    Σοὶ χάρις, ὦ πάντων βασιλεῦ, πάντων δὲ ποιητά.
    Οὐρανὸς ἐπλήσθη δόξης σέο, πᾶσά τε γαῖα
    Σῆς σοφίης. Θεὸς Υἱὸς ὁ σὸς Λόγος ἔκτισε πάντα.

⁵³προσώπου PG.
⁵⁴βυθὸν PG.

530 eminent ugliness of the face, storm of the heart,
drunken gadfly who drive men off cliffs and send them to
      Tartarus.
O legion of spirits, evil composite,[48]
who tear up bonds and fetters with their shackles,[49] Christ
      wants you,
the one whom the whole world cannot support,
535 who himself governs all without stumbling,
ruling the life of mortals and angels,
who brings release from evil spirits and
passions, to those who call on him intently;
he himself wants you to flee as quickly as possible from here.
540 Go out and fill the depths of your swine.
They will readily receive you as you cast yourself into the sea.[50]
Depart from all of us who are dear to God.
      All this is from my period of silence. But you who have
      suppressed my speech,[51]
if you have uttered a word worthy of what is here contained,
545 utter it to me. But if it's worthy of silence, it does not matter to
      me.
And I will bind my ears to words spoken to me, as I've bound
      my mouth to speaking.

I.1.33. Thanksgiving (PG 37.514)

Thanks be to you, O king of all and maker of all.
The heavens are filled with your glory and all the earth
with your wisdom. God the Word, your Son, created all things.

---

[48]Mk 5.9.

[49]Mk 5.4.

[50]Mt 8.30–32; Mk 5.11–13; Lk 8.32–34.

[51]Gregory means the bishops who ordered him to resign from the See of Constantinople in 381; Oberhaus, *Gegen den Zorn*, 193.

Σὸν ἅγιον Πνεῦμα ζωὴν πάντεσσι χορηγεῖ.
5   Ἰλήκοις κόσμῳ θεία Τριάς· ἵλαθι δ' ἡμῖν,
Υἱὲ Θεοῦ κατὰ πνεῦμα, καὶ ἀνθρώπου κατὰ σάρκα,
Ὅστις ἐπὶ σταυροῖο μόρον τέτληκας ἐπισπεῖν,
Οἷα βροτός· τριτάτη δὲ πύλας λίπες ἀϊδονῆος,
Οἷα Θεός· θανάτου γὰρ ἔλυσας δεσμὸν ἀναστάς,
10   Καὶ βροτέῃ γενεῇ φύσιν ὤπασας, οἷα καὶ ἡμᾶς
Ζώειν ἤματα πάντα, σὲ δ' ἄμβροτον αἰὲν ἀείδειν.

I.1.34. Εὐχαριστήριον ἄλλο. (*dubium* PG 37.515–517)

Σοὶ χάρις, ὦ πάντων βασιλεῦ, πάντων δὲ ποιητά.
Σοὶ χάρις· ὃς τὰ νοητὰ λόγῳ, τά θ' ὁρατὰ κελεύσει
Στῆσας τ' οὐ πρὶν ἐόντα, καὶ ἐξ ἀφανοῦς κατέδειξας.
Σὸν θρόνον ἀμφιέπουσιν ἀκήρατοι ὑμνητῆρες,
5   Ἔνθεν μυριάδες, καὶ χιλιάδες πάλιν ἔνθεν,
Ἀγγελικῆς στρατιῆς πυρόεις χορός, ἄφθιτοι ἀρχὴν
Λαοὶ πρωτοτόκων, καὶ λαμπομένων χορὸς ἄστρων·
Πνεύματα θεσπεσίων ἀνδρῶν, ψυχαί τε δικαίων,
Πάντες ὁμηγερέες, καὶ σὸν θρόνον ἀμφιέποντες,
10   Γηθοσύνῃ τε, φόβῳ τε διηνεκὲς ἀείδουσι
Ὕμνον ἀνυμνείοντες ἀκήρατον, ἢ καὶ ἄπαυστον·
Σοὶ χάρις, ὦ πάντων βασιλεῦ, πάντων δὲ ποιητά.
Οὗτος ἀκήρατος ὕμνος ἐπ' οὐρανίοιο χοροῖο.
Ναὶ λίτομαι κἀγώ, Πάτερ ἄφθιτε, καὶ γόνυ κάμπτω

Your Holy Spirit bestows life on all.
5 Divine Trinity, may you be gracious to the world. Hearken to
    us,
Son of God according to the spirit and Son of man according
    to the flesh,
who undertook to suffer death on the Cross,
as a mortal; but on the third day you quit the gates of Hades
as God. For having risen you loosed the bond of death,
10 and you conferred to the mortal race a nature by which we
    might
live all days, and sing to you, Immortal One, always.

I.1.34. Thanksgiving (PG 37.515–517)

Thanks be to you, O king of all and maker of all.
Thanks be to you, who established the intelligible by your
    word,
and the visible by your command, things which previously
    were not, and you made them known from what was
    hidden.
A choir inviolate surrounds your throne
5 where there are thousands and more myriads,
a fiery chorus of an angelic army, a people uncorrupted
from the beginning of the first born, and a chorus of brilliant
    stars,
the spirits of holy men and the souls of the just,
all of them assembled together and circling your throne,
10 singing unceasingly in gladness and in fear
offering up a perfect and ceaseless hymn.
Thanks be to you, O king of all and maker of all.
Such is the perfect hymn from the celestial chorus.
Indeed I beseech you, incorruptible Father, and I bend the knee

15 Ἡμετέρης κραδίης, Πάτερ ἄμβροτε, καὶ νόος ἔνδον   [516]
    Πρηνὴς σου προπάροιθε· κάρη δέ μοι ἐς χθόνα νεύει
    Λισσομένῳ· κεῖμαι δ᾽ ἱκέτης, καὶ δάκρυα χεύω.
    Οὐδὲ γὰρ ἄξιός εἰμι πρὸς οὐρανὸν ἀντία λεύσσειν
    Ἀλλὰ σύ μ᾽ οἰκτείροις, ἐλέους Πάτερ, ἵλαος ἔσσο
20 Σῷ κινυρῷ θεράποντι· σάου δέ με χεῖρα τανύσσας
    Ἐξ ὀνύχων θανάτοιο, νοήματα πάντα καθήρας.
    Μή μ᾽ ἀπογυμνώσῃς σοῦ Πνεύματος, ἀλλ᾽ ἔτι μᾶλλον
    Χεῦε μένος καὶ θάρσος ἐνὶ στήθεσσιν ἐμοῖσιν·
    Ὄφρα σε καὶ κραδίῃ, καὶ χείλεσι καλὸν ἀείσω.
25 Ὥσπερ ἐμῷ γενετῆρι, σῷ θεράποντι παρέστης,
    Δὸς καὶ ἐμοὶ καθαρὸν βίοτον, καθαράν τε τελευτήν,
    Ἐλπωρήν τε τυχεῖν ἀγαθήν, ἔλεόν τε, χάριν τε·
    Πάντα δ᾽ ἀμαλδύνει, ὅσα ἤλιτον ἐκ νεότητος,
    Ὡς ἀγαθὸς βασιλεύς· ὅτι σοὶ χάρις ἤματα πάντα,   [517]
30 Σοὶ χάρις ἤματα πάντα, καὶ εἰς αἰῶνας ἅπαντας.

II.1.20. Νοσοῦντος εὐχὴ πρὸς Χριστόν. (PG 37.1279)

Πῆξόν με, Χριστέ· πῶς ἐλύθη σὸς λάτρις;
Ὑμνῳδὸς ἀργεῖ γλῶσσα. Πῶς φέρεις τόδε;
Ἀλλ᾽ ἅρμοσόν με, μὴ πρόῃ τὸν σὸν θύτην.
Ποθῶ πάλιν στῆναί τε καὶ σωτηρίας
5 Κῆρυξ γενέσθαι, καὶ λαὸν καθαγνίσαι·
Σὺ τὸ σθένος μου, λίσσομαι, μή μ᾽ ἐκλίπῃς.
Εἴ σ᾽ ἐν ζάλῃ προύδωκα, βαλοίμην ἔτι.

15 of my heart, immortal Father, and my inner mind
    lies prostrate before you. I bow my head to the ground
    in supplication. I lie down as a suppliant and pour out tears.
    For I am not worthy to look up to heaven.
    But have mercy on me, Father of mercy, be propitious
20 to your whimpering servant. Stretch out your hand to me
    in the jaws of death, cleanse all my thoughts.
    Do not strip me of your Spirit, but ever more pour
    strength and perseverance into my breast,
    that I may sing you rightly with my heart and with my lips.
25 Just as you had been present to my father be present to me
        your servant,
    give me as well a pure life and a pure end,
    to have good hope and mercy and grace.
    Like a generous king, blot out all the sins that I have committed
    from my youth. So that thanks may be to you all days,
30 thanks be to you all days, even unto the ages of ages.

II.1.20. Prayer of a sick man to Christ (PG 37.1279)

Strengthen me, Christ. How is it that your servant has been
        ruined?
My tongue slackens from its praising. How can you bear this?
But set me straight; do not reject your priest.
I yearn to stand again and to be a herald
        of salvation, and to sanctify your people.
5 You are my strength; I beg you, do not forsake me.
If I ever betrayed you in the storm, may I be tossed about
        again.

II.1.22. Ἱκετήριον. (PG 37.1281–1282)

Χριστὲ, φάος μερόπων, πυρόει στύλε Γρηγορίοιο
Ψυχῇ, πλαζομένῃ πικρῆς βιότου δι' ἐρήμης,
Σχὲς Φαραὼ κακόμητιν, ἀναιδέας ἐργοδιώκτας·
Καὶ πηλοῦ μ' ἀδέτοιο, καὶ Αἰγύπτοιο βαρείης
5   Ἐξερύσαις, πληγῇσιν ἀεικελίῃσι δαμάσσας
Δυσμενέας, λείην δὲ πόροις ὁδόν. Ἢν δὲ κίχησιν
Ἐχθρὸς ἐπισπέρχων, σὺ δέ μοι καὶ πόντον ἐρυθρὸν
Τμήξειας, στερεὴν δὲ διεκπεράοιμι θάλασσαν,
Σπεύδων ἐς χθόνα δῖαν, ἐμὸν λάχος, ὥσπερ ὑπέστης·
10   Καὶ ποταμοὺς στήσειας ἀπείρονας, ἀλλοφύλων τε
Κλίναις θούριον ἔγχος, ἀγάστονον. Εἰ δ' ἐπιβαίην
Γῆς ἱερῆς, μέλψω σε διηνεκέεσσιν ἐν ὕμνοις.
Χριστὲ ἄναξ, τί με σαρκὸς ἐν ἄρκυσι ταῖσδ' ἐνέδησας;
Τίπτε βίῳ κρυόεντι, καὶ ἰλυόεντι βερέθρῳ,
15   Εἰ ἐτεὸν θεός εἰμι, λάχος δὲ σὸν, ὥσπερ ἄκουσα;   [1282]
Ἐκ μέν μοι μελέων σθένος ὤλετο, οὐ δέ τι γοῦνα
Ἕσπεται· ἀλλά μ' ἔλυσε χρόνος, καὶ νοῦσος ἀνιγρὴ,
Τηκεδάνη τε μέριμνα, φίλοι τ' ἄφιλα φρονέοντες.
Εἴκειν δ' οὐκ ἐθέλουσιν ἁμαρτάδες, ἀλλ' ἔτι μᾶλλον
20   Στείβουσ' ἀδρανέοντα, κύνες δ' ὡς πτῶκα λαγωὸν,
Ἢ κεμάδ' ἀμφὶς ἔχουσι, λιλαιόμενοι κορέσασθαι.
Ἢ στῆσον κακότητα καὶ ἵλαθι, ἤ μ' ὑποδέξαι
Δηρὸν ἀεθλεύοντα, καὶ ἄλγεσι μέτρον ἐπέστω,
Ἢ λήθης νέφος ἐσθλὸν ἐμὰς φρένας ἀμφικαλύπτοι.

II.1.22. Supplication (PG 37.1281–1282)

Christ, light of mortals, the column who burns in Gregory's
soul, which wanders through the bitter desert of life,
subdue the evil-plotting Pharoah, and his impudent
  taskmasters.
Snatch me from the slippery mud, and from burdensome
  Egypt,
5   casting down the enemies with unseemly blows,
and make the way smooth. But if the enemy
should overtake me in pursuit, may you also split the Red Sea
for me, and may I pass through the stiffened sea,
hastening for brilliant land, my inheritance, just as you swore.
10   And still the boundless rivers, and you might turn back
the hostile sword of rival tribes, which we bemoan. But if
I should go up to the holy land, I will sing to you with ceaseless
  hymns.
Christ the king, why did you bind me with these snares of
  flesh?
Why am I in this frigid life and this miry pit,
15   if I am truly God, your inheritance, as I have heard?
The strength vanishes from my limbs, and my knees
do not obey me. But time and woeful illness have destroyed
  me,
and idle anxiety, and friends contriving unfriendly acts.
But sinners refuse to yield, and still more they
20   trample down the weak man, like dogs when they surround
a fearful hare or deer, eager to eat their fill.
Either put an end to my evil and have mercy, or receive me
having wrestled too long, and put a limit on my pains,
or may a welcome cloud of forgetting envelop my heart.

II.1.24. Εὐχὴ ἑωθινή. (PG 37.1284)

Ὄρθρος δίδωμι τῷ Θεῷ μου δεξιὰς,
Μηδὲν σκοτῶδες ἢ δράσειν ἢ αἰνέσειν,
Ἀλλ᾽ ὡς μάλιστά σοι θύσειν τὴν ἡμέραν,
Μένων ἄσειστος, καὶ παθῶν αὐτοκράτωρ.
5 Αἰσχύνομαι τὸ γῆρας, ἂν κάκιστος ὦ,
Καὶ τὴν τράπεζαν ἧς παραστάτης ἐγώ.
Ὁρμὴ μὲν αὕτη, Χριστέ μου· σὺ δ᾽ εὐόδου.

II.1.25. Πρὸς ἑσπέραν θρῆνος. (PG 37.1285)

Ἐψευσάμην σε. τὴν ἀλήθειαν, Λόγε,
Σοὶ τὴν παροῦσαν ἡμέραν καθαγνίσας.
Οὐ πάντα φωτεινόν με νὺξ ἐδέξατο.
Ἦ μὴν προσηυξάμην τε καὶ τοῦτ᾽ ᾠόμην·
5 Ἀλλ᾽ ἔστιν οὗ μοι καὶ προσέπταισαν πόδες.
Ζόφος γὰρ ἦλθε βάσκανος σωτηρίας.
Λάμποις τὸ φῶς μοι, Χριστέ, καὶ πάλιν φανείς.

II.1.27. Θρῆνος. (PG 37.1286–1287)

Αἲ αἲ τῶν παθέων! Τίπτ᾽ ἤλιτον; ἢ ἄρα μοῦνος
Σῶν καθαρῶν θυέων ἅπτομαι οὐχ ὁσίως;
Ἦ με πυροῖς παθέεσσι, καθάρσιε, ἢ τύφον ἄλλων
Ἴσχεις, ἤ με φέρεις γυμνὸν ἐπ᾽ ἀντιπάλῳ;
5 Ταῦτα μὲν αὐτὸς, ἄναξ, νωμᾷς, Λόγε. Αὐτὰρ ἔγωγε
Βαιὸν ὑπὲρ γαίης ἄσθμα φέρω πύματον.
Δάκρυα πάντ᾽ ἐκένωσα, γόος δέ μοι ἔργον ἐτύχθη.

II.1.24. Morning prayer (PG 37.1284)

In the morning I give my right hand to God,
to offer and praise nothing shadowy,
but as much as possible to sacrifice the day to you,
that remaining unshaken, I may be master of my passions.
5   If I should be utterly wicked I would shame my old age
and also the altar that I attend.
This is my desire, my Christ. Guide me straight.

II.1.25. Lament at evening (PG 37.1285)

I have deceived you who are the truth, Logos,
although I consecrated the present day to you.
Night has not received me fully brilliant.
Most truly I vowed and believed this.
5   But somewhere even my feet have stumbled.
For darkness, an assailant of my salvation, has come.
May you shine your light on me, Christ, as you appear once
       again.

II.1.27. Lament (PG 37.1286–1287)

Woe, woe for my sufferings! Where have I gone wrong? O, am
       I then
the only one who handles your pure sacrifices unworthily?
Or is it you, O purifier, who try me by the fire of sufferings, or
       keep me from
the vanity of others, or bear me naked against an enemy?
5   You alone, Lord, direct these matters. But I offer up
a scanty final breath upon the earth.
I have spent my last tear, and wailing has become my chore.

Μέχρι τίνος παλάμαις κείμεθ᾽ ἐν ἀσεβέων;
Ἀλλὰ, μάκαρ, στῆσόν με, καὶ εἰ κακὸν, ἀλλ᾽ ἱερῆα,
10   Μή τις ὀλισθήσῃ πήμασιν ἡμετέροις.
Ὤλετο εὖχος ἔμοιγε, καὶ ἄλγεα σαρκὸς ὄλοιτο.   [1287]
Οἴχετ᾽ Ἀναστασίη, λῆγε καὶ, ἀμπλακίη.
Αἳ αἳ δάκρυά μοι καταλείβεται, ἔνδοθεν ἦτορ
Παχνοῦται· διπλὴν νοῦσον ἐπίσχες, ἄναξ·
15   Νοῦσον ἐπίσχες, ἄναξ, διολώλαμεν. Ἢ ἄρα μούνῳ
Οἶκτος ἀπεκλείσθη σῷ λάτρι Γρηγορίῳ;
Τέτρωμαι πολλοῖσι κακοῖς καὶ ἄλγεσι σαρκός·
Σοὶ δὲ, Χριστὲ, χάρις, ὅς με πυροῖς πάθεσιν.
Ἢ στῆσον κακότητα, καὶ ἵλαθι σῷ θεράποντι,
20   Ἢ τὸ δίδου θυμῷ τλήμονι πάντα φέρειν.

II.1.28. Ἐλεγειακόν. (PG 37.1287–1288)

Ὄλβιος ὅστις ἄσαρκον ἔχει βίον, οὐδ᾽ ἐπίμικτον
Εἰκόνι τῇ μεγάλῃ βόρβορον ἀμφέθετο.
Παῦρα μὲν οὐρανίοισι νοήμασιν ἔσπετ᾽ ἀνάγκη,   [1288]
Πλείονα δ᾽ ἀντιάει, καὶ ζόφος ἐστὶ νόου.
5   Εἰ ῥοίης γένος εἰμὶ, τί μ᾽ ἀθανάτοισιν ἐΐσκεις,
Εἰ πνεύσθην θεόθεν, τίπτε με πηλόδετον,
Χριστὲ, φέρεις; γῆρας μὲν ἔβη, καὶ ἅψε᾽ ἀκιδνά·
Ἡ δ᾽ ἔτι λύσσαν ἔχει σὰρξ ἐπανισταμένη
Ἀμφαδὸν, ἢ λοχόωσα· τὸ δ᾽ ἄλγιον, ὁππότε μύστην
10   Οὐρανίων θυέων μὴ καθαρὸν παρέχει.
Ὁρκίζω σε Θεοῖο μέγα κράτος, ἠδὲ κελαινὸν
Ἦμαρ ἀλιτροβίων, ἴσχεο μαργοσύνης.

How long shall I be held by the hands of the wicked?
But you, blessed one, strengthen me, even if I am evil (but still
    a priest),
10 so that no one be corrupted by my failures.
For my boast has vanished, so may the pain of my flesh vanish.
Anastasia is abandoned;[52] cease, likewise, wickedness.
Woe, woe, my tears flow forth, and my inner heart
hardens. Ward off a double sickness, Lord.
15 Ward off a sickness, Lord, lest we be ruined. Or is mercy
shut off from your servant Gregory alone?
I am wounded by many evils and pains of the flesh.
But praise to you, Christ, who would try me by the fire of
    sufferings.
Either stop evil and have mercy on your servant,
20 or grant his wretched spirit to endure all things.

II.1.28. Elegiac (PG 37.1287–1288)

Happy the man who leads a life free of the flesh and does not
    cover
his great image with a mixture of filth.
Seldom and only when forced does one pursue heavenly
    thoughts,
but more often he opposes them, and his mind is darkness.
5 If I am born of flux, why do you make me like immortals;
if I have breathed from God, why do you leave me,
Christ, earth-bound? Old age advances, my limbs are weak.
But the indomitable flesh still shows madness
publicly, or lies in wait. And this is more painful,
10 when it offers an impure mystery of the heavenly sacrifices.
I swear to you, by the great power of God, and by the day
that is the doom of the wicked, restrain your wantonness.

[52]That is, his church in Constantinople.

II.1.31. Πόθος τοῦ θανάτου. (PG 37.1299-1300)

Δὶς, οἶδα τοῦτο, φεῦ! δὶς ἐπτερνισμένος·
Εἰ μὲν δικαίως, προσδέχοιθ᾽ ὑμᾶς Θεός·
Εἰ δ᾽ οὐ δικαίως, προσδέχοιθ᾽ ὅμως Θεός·
Οὐδὲν γὰρ ὑμῶν οὐδὲ ὧς καθέξομαι.   [1300]
5   Πλὴν ἐκλέλοιπα, καὶ ποθῶ λύσιν κακῶν.
Τῶν μὲν παρόντων εἰμὶ πάντων ἔμπλεως,
Πλούτου, πενίας, χαρμονῶν, οὐ χαρμονῶν,
Δόξης, ἀτιμίας τε, δυσμενῶν, φίλων·
Τῶν δ᾽ οὐ παρόντων εὔχομαι πεῖραν λαβεῖν.
10 Πέρας λόγου· τολμῶ δὲ, καὶ δέχου λόγον·
Εἰ μηδέν εἰμι, Χριστέ μου, τίς ἡ πλάσις;
Εἰ τίμιός σοι, πῶς τόσοις ἐλαύνομαι;

II.1.42. Θρῆνος διὰ τῶν αὐτοῦ μόγων, καὶ πρὸς Χριστὸν δέησις
περὶ λύσεως τοῦ αὐτοῦ βίου. (PG 37.1344–1346)

Γαῖα φίλη, καὶ Πόντε, πάτρης πέδον ἀλλοδαπῆς τε,
Καὶ νεότης, πολιή τε βίου δύσι, καὶ πτερόεντες
Μῦθοι, μόχθε περισσὲ, καὶ οὓς τέκε Πνεῦμα φαεινὸν,
Καὶ πτόλιες, σκόπελοί τε, ἐμὸν σκέπας, ὧν διὰ πάντων
5   Ἤλυθον, ἰσχανόων Χριστοῦ θεότητι πελάσσαι,
Πῶς μοῦνος τρηχεῖαν ἔβην ὁδὸν ἔνθα καὶ ἔνθα,
Στρωφῶν ἀργαλέοιο βίου τύπον, οὐδ᾽ ἐδυνάσθην
Οὐδ᾽ ὅσον ἔν ποτ᾽ ἐλαφρὸν ἐπὶ χθονὸς ἴχνος ἐρεῖσαι,
Ἀλλ᾽ αἰεί με μόγοισι μόγοι πέμπουσι κακοῖσιν;

II.1.31. Desire for Death (PG 37.1299–1300)

Twice, I know it. Alas! twice I've been deceived.
If justly, may God await you;
if unjustly, may God await you still.
For I won't prevail over you at all even in this way.
5   Rather I have utterly failed and I long for release from evils.
For I am stuffed full of all that the present offers,
of wealth, poverty, joys, things that bring no joy,
honor, humiliation, enemies, and friends;
yet I pray that I might experience things not present.
10 The end of this account; I am bold, but receive my speech.
If I am nothing, my Christ, why did you form me thus?
If I am precious to you, how am I pressed by so many evils?

II.1.42. Lament about his pains, and a prayer to Christ about release from life (PG 37.1344–1346)

Dear homeland and Pontus,[53] the soil of paternal and foreign
   land,
and youth, and the graying of life as it sets, and discourses both
winged (a tiresome waste) and those that the brilliant Spirit
   bore,[54]
and cities, and cliffs, my refuge, through all of which
5   I have arrived, desiring to approach the divinity of Christ,
how have I alone traveled the rough road here and there,
winding through this type of a harsh life, and I have not been
   able
to fix at any point one meager step upon the earth,
but distress always sends me into evil distress?

---

[53]The region of northern Asia Minor.
[54]I.e., profane and Christian litterature.

10   Ὦ σοφίη, σὺ δίδαξον ὅθεν τόσον ἄχθος ἔμοιγε.   [1345]
Πῶς μόγος εὐσεβέεσσι, καὶ οὐ μόγος ὀλλυμένοισιν;
Ἦ ῥά τις ἀμπλακίης ποινὴ τάδε, ἤ ῥα βίοιο
Ἄνθρακες, ὡς χρυσοῖο καθαιρομένου χοάνοισιν;
Ἦ ῥά μ' ὁ λυσσώδης καὶ βάσκανος, οἵά τιν' Ἰώβ,
15   Ἐς δῆριν καλέει; Σὺ δ' ἀλείφατι σόν με παλαιστὴν
Τρίψας, εὖ τε πάροιθε μέγαν γυμνοῖς πρὸς ἀγῶνα,
Ὡς κεν ἀεθλεύσαντι γέρας καὶ κῦδος ὀπάσσῃς;
Ταῦτα μὲν αὐτός, ἄναξ, οἶδας, Λόγε. Καὶ γὰρ ἅπαντα
Κόσμον ἄγεις, μεγάλοισι λόγοις κρυπτοῖσιν ἑλίσσων,
20   Ὧν ὀλίγη τις πάμπαν ἐς ἡμέας ἔρχεται αὐγὴ,
Πηλὸν ἔτ' εἰλυμένους, καὶ ὄμματα νωθρὰ φέροντας.
Αὐτὰρ ἐγὼ κέκμηκα βίῳ, τυτθὸν δ' ἐπὶ γαίης
Ἄσθμα φέρω, πολλῇσιν ἐλαυνόμενος κακότησι,   [1346]
Δυσμενέων, φιλίων τε, τὸ καὶ περιώσιον ἄλγος.
25   Τοὔνεκεν αἰάζω, πίπτω δ' ὑπὸ γούνασι σεῖο.
Δὸς λῦσιν βιότοιο νεκρῷ σέο. Δὸς καμάτοιο
Ἄμπνευσιν, ζωῆς δέ μ' ἐλαφροτέρης ἐπίβησον,
Ἧς χάριν ἀσχαλόω, καὶ κήδεα μυρί' ἀνέτλην.
Ἀγγελικοῖς δὲ χοροῖσι φέρων πελάσειας ὁδίτην
30   Οὐρανίου πυλεῶνος, ὅθι κλέος ἀστράπτοντος
Τρισσοῖς ἐν φαέεσσιν ἑνὸς μεγάλοιο Θεοῖο.

10 O Wisdom, teach me whence such great toil comes to me.
    Why is there trouble for the pious, and no trouble for the
        wicked?
    Or is this some penalty for sin, or some purifying fire for
    a life, like the furnaces where gold is refined?
    Or has the raging and envious one called me into battle,
15 as he did to Job? But will you then rub me with oil
    as an athlete, once you have stripped me for the great struggle,
    in order to furnish a reward and honor for me in my clash?
    But you know this for yourself, Logos. For you rule
    the whole universe, binding it together with great and hidden
        words,
20 from which some little gleam reaches us complete,
    as we still trudge in the mire and bear downcast eyes.
    But I am wearied by life, and I bear a tiny breath
    on the earth, cast about by many evils,
    the surrounding pain from enemies, and even worse, from
        friends.
25 Therefore I cry out and fall at your knees.
    By your death give me freedom from this life. Give me
    rest from my trouble, and lead me up to easier life,
    for whose sake I toil and bear numberless labors.
    May you draw me into the heavenly gate bearing me, a
        wayfarer,
30 among the angelic choirs, where there is the glory
    of one great God flashing forth in triple rays.

II.1.43. Πρὸς ἑαυτὸν κατὰ πεῦσιν καὶ ἀπόκρισιν.
(PG 37.1346–1349)

Ποῦ δὲ λόγοι πτερόεντες; ἐς ἠέρα. Ποῦ νεότητος
Ἄνθος ἐμῆς; διόλωλε. Τὸ δὲ κλέος; ᾤχετ᾽ ἄϊστον.
Ποῦ σθένος εὐπαγέων μελέων; κατὰ νοῦσος ἔκαμψε.   [1347]
Ποῦ κτῆσις καὶ πλοῦτος; ἔχει Θεός. Ἄλλα δ᾽ ἀλιτρῶν
5 Ἁρπαλέαις παλάμῃσι πόρε φθόνος. Οἱ δὲ τοκῆες,
Ἠδὲ κασιγνήτων ἱερὴ δυάς; ἐς τάφον ἦλθον.
Μούνη μοι πάτρη περιλείπετο· ἀλλ᾽ ἄρα καὶ τῆς,
Ὄρσας οἶδμα κελαινὸν, ὁ βάσκανος ἤλασε δαίμων.
Καὶ νῦν ξεῖνος, ἔρημος ἐπ᾽ ἀλλοτρίης ἀλάλημαι,
10 Ἕλκων ζωήν τε λυπρὴν, καὶ γῆρας ἀφαυρὸν,
Ἄθρονος, ἀπτολίεθρος, ἄπαις, τεκέεσσι μεμηλὼς,
Ζώων ἦμαρ ἐπ᾽ ἦμαρ ἀειπλανέεσσι πόδεσσι.
Ποῖ ῥίψω τόδε σῶμα; τί μοι τέλος ἀντιβολήσει;
Τίς γῆ, τίς δὲ τάφος με φιλόξενος ἀμφικαλύψει;
15 Τίς δ᾽ ὄσσοις μινύθουσιν ἐμοῖς ἐπὶ δάκτυλα θήσει,
Ἤ ῥά τις εὐσεβέων, Χριστοῦ φίλος, ἢ ῥα κάκιστος;   [1348]
Ταῦτα μὲν αὖρα φέροι. Τυτθῆς φρενὸς ἥδε μεληδών,
Εἴ τε τάφῳ δώσει τις ἐμὸν δέμας, ἄπνοον ἄχθος,
Εἴ τε καὶ ἀκτερέϊστον ἕλωρ θήρεσσι γένοιτο,
20 Θήρεσιν, ἠὲ κύνεσσιν ἑλώριον, ἢ πετεηνοῖς,
Εἰ δ᾽ ἐθέλεις, πυρίκαυστον ἐς ἠέρα χείρεσι πάσσοις,
Ἠὲ κατὰ σκοπέλων μεγάλων ῥίψειας ἄτυμβον,

II.1.43. To himself in the form of question and answer
(PG 37.1346–1349)

Where then are my winged words? In thin air. Where is the
    bloom
of my youth? Lost. Where is my fame? It has left, unseen.
Where is the strength of my well-formed limbs? Worn out by
    sickness.
Where are my possessions and wealth? God has them. But
    greed
5   supplies the grabbing hands of sinners. And my parents,
and my two holy siblings? They've entered the tomb.
Only my homeland is left for me. But even thence
a deceiving demon drives me out, raising up a dire storm,
and now a stranger and alone, I wander in a foreign land,
10   leading a sorry life, and a feeble old age,
without a throne, without a city, childless, but worried about
    my children,[55]
living from day to day on ever-wandering feet.
Where shall I toss my body? What end will meet me?
Which land, which hospitable grave will house me?
15   Who will place his finger on my diminishing eyes,
will he be one of the pious, a friend of Christ, or evil?
Let the breeze carry off this care. This is the worry of a paltry
    spirit,
that if someone should lay my body, a breathless burden, in the
    grave,
or if it go unburied as prey for beasts,
20   for beasts, as prey for dogs or birds;
or if you wish, you might sprinkle the ashes into the air with
    your hands,
or you might cast it unburied from a cliff,

[55]I.e., the Christians of his congregation.

Ἢ ποταμοῖσι πύθοιτο, καὶ ὑετίῃσι ῥοῇσιν
Οὐ γὰρ ἄϊστος ἐγὼ μόνος ἔσσομαι, οὐδ' ἀσύνακτος.
25 Ὡς ὄφελον! πολλοῖς τόδε λώϊον. Ἀλλ' ἅμα πάντας
Ὕστατον ἦμαρ ἄγει περάτων ἄπο, νεύμασι θείοις,
Εἴ που καὶ σποδιή τις, ὀλωλότα θ' ἄψεα νούσῳ.
Ἓν δὲ τόδ' αἰάζω, καὶ δείδια βῆμα Θεοῖο,
Καὶ ποταμοὺς πυρόεντας, ἀφεγγέα τ' αἰνὰ βέρεθρα   [1349]
30 Χριστὲ ἄναξ, σὺ δέ μοι πάτρη, σθένος, ὄλβος, ἅπαντα.
Σοὶ δ' ἄρ' ἀναψύξαιμι, βίον καὶ κῆδε' ἀμείψας.

II.1.49. Θρῆνος. (PG 37.1384)

Ὤμοι ἐγών, ὅτι δή με πρὸς οὐρανὸν ἠδὲ Θεοῖο
Χῶρον ἐπειγόμενον, σῶμα τόδ' ἀμφὶς ἔχει!
Οὐδέ πη ἔκβασίς ἐστι πολυπλανέος βιότοιο,   [1385]
Καὶ στυγερῆς κακίης, ἥ μ' ἐπέδησε κάτω,
5 Πάντοθεν ἀπροφάτοισι περικτυπέουσα μερίμναις,
Βοσκομέναις ψυχῆς κάλλεα καὶ χάριτας.
Ἀλλά με λῦσον, Ἄναξ, λῦσον χθονίων ἀπὸ δεσμῶν,
Καί με χοροστασίην τάξον ἐς οὐρανίην.

II.1.50. Κατὰ τοῦ πονηροῦ εἰς τὴν νόσον. (PG 37.1385–1393)

Ἤλυθες αὖθις ἔμοιγε, δολοπλόκε ὡς ἐνοήθης,
Βένθος ἐμῆς κραδίης ἔνδοθι βοσκόμενος,
Καὶ πολλοῖς κρατεροῖς τε τινάγμασι τοῦδε βίοιο,
Εἰκόνα τὴν ἱερὴν γνὺξ βαλέειν ποθέων·

or it might be heard to be in the rivers, and to the flowing
  waters
I will not alone be unseen or outcast.
25 O, would that it would happen! This would be better for many.
  But
  the last day brings all together from the limits of the world, by
    divine commands,
  even if one is ashes, his limbs destroyed by sickness.
  I lament this alone: namely the dire judgment seat of God,
  and the fiery rivers, and the horrible lightless pits.
30 Christ the Lord, you are my homeland, my strength, my
    wealth, my all.
  Exchanging my troubles for life, may I be refreshed in you.

II.1.49. Lament (PG 38.1384)

Woe is me, since this body surrounds and holds me back from
hastening towards God's heavenly dwelling.
And there is no escape from this much-deceiving life,
and from hateful evil, which bound me here below,
5 from every side they fall upon me with unforeseen anxieties,
devouring the lovely grace of my soul.
But free me, Lord, free me from earthly chains,
and set me in the heavenly choir.

II.1.50. Against the deceiver in time of sickness (PG 37.1385–1393)

You have come to me again, a deceiver (as you've been
  detected)
to devour the inner depths of my heart,
and through the many, greater disturbances of this life,
eager to force the holy image to bend the knee.

5   Σαρξὶν ἐρισθενέεσσιν ἐνήλαο, καί μ' ἐδάϊξας
    Εἰς πόδας ἐκ κεφαλῆς, ῥεύματι δεσμὰ λύσας
    Τῷ ξηρὴν ἐδίηνε Θεὸς φύσιν, ὡς ἐκέρασσε   [1386]
    Τῇ ψυχρῇ λιαρὴν κοσμογόνῳ σοφίῃ,
    Ὡς κεν ἰσοστασίη δέμας ἄρτιον ἅμα φυλάσσοι,
10 Τὴν δὲ διχοστασίην καὶ βιότοιο φύγω.
    Ἦλυθες ἀνδροφόνοισι νοήμασιν, ἐς δ' ἐμέ, τλῆμον,
    Σῆς δνοφερῆς κακίης ἰὸν ἔχευσας ὅλον.
    Οὐχ ἅλις ἦεν ἔμοιγε βαρύστονα γήραος ἕλκειν
    Ἄλγεα, καὶ σκοπέλων ἄχθεα τρινακρίων·
15 Ἀλλά με καὶ στυγερὴ κατεδάσσατο δάπτρια νοῦσος,
    Τηκεδανὴ μελέων, εἰς ἔτος ἐξ ἔτεος.
    Τοῖσιν ἐπαιάζω, καὶ στείνομαι, ὡς ὅτε τις λὶς
    Ἄλκιμος, ἐμπλεχθεὶς ἄρκυσι θηροφόνων.
    Οὐ μύθων ποθέω σκιρτήματα, οὐκ ἐρατεινὴν
20 Πᾶσιν ὁμηλικίην, οὔτε μὲν εὐθαλίην,
    Οὐκ ἀγορὰς πολίων, οὐκ ἄλσεα, οὐδὲ λοετρά,   [1387]
    Οὐδ' ὅσα τοῦ δολεροῦ ἄνθεα τοῦδε βίου.
    Ταῦτα γὰρ οὐδὲ πάροιθεν ἐμοὶ φίλα, ἐξότε Χριστὸν
    Ἀγκασάμην, χθονίων τῆλ' ἀπανιστάμενος.
25 Αἰάζω δ' ὅτι με Χριστοῦ μεγάλοιο λέλοιπεν
    Ὄμμα ζωοφόρον, ᾧ μέλον, εἴποτ' ἔην,
    Ὅς με καὶ ἐν σπλάγχνοισιν ἁγνῆς κύδηνε τεκούσης,
    Καὶ πόντου κρυεροῦ ῥύσατο, καὶ παθέων.
    Αἰάζω λαοῖο θεόφρονος ἡνία ῥίψας,
30 Οὐ μὲν ἀπορρίψας, οὔτι δὲ χερσὶ φέρων·
    Ὅς πρόσθεν μύθοισιν ἀγάλλετο ἡμετέροισιν,
    Ἡνίκ' ἀπὸ γλώσσης τρισσὸν ἔλαμπε σέλας.
    Νῦν γε μὲν, ὡς λιπόμαστος ἐν ἀγκαλίδεσσι τεκούσης
    Νηπίαχος θηλὴν ἔσπασεν αὐαλέην

5   You trampled on me even as my flesh struggled, and smote me
    from head to foot; you have loosed the bond of the fluid
    with which God moistened a dry nature, when he mixed
        warmth
    with cold according to his world-generating wisdom,
    so that a balance binds together my bodily form,
10 and that I avoid all the imbalance of this life.
    You have come with murderous designs against me, O you
        wretch,
    and poured out all the venom of your dusky evil.
    I do not have enough to draw along the groaning pains
    of old age, even like the burdens of the Sicilian heights.[56]
15 But indeed a hateful sickness devours me in destruction,
    a wasting away of my limbs, from year to year.
    Because of these I cry out and groan, as when a valiant
    lion is trapped in the snares of the hunters.
    I do not long for the joys of speeches, or loving
20 companionship with everyone, or blooming youth,
    or city centers, or groves, or baths,
    or however many blossoms there are in this bitter life.
    For these have never been dear to me
    since I embraced Christ, abandoning earthly things.
25 I cry out then since the enlivening eye of
    great Christ has left me, who once cared for me,
    who once ennobled me in the womb of a holy mother,
    and freed me from the icy sea and from the passions.
    I cry out, for I have dropped the reins of a holy people,
30 not tossing them aside, but not holding them in my hands,
    those who once rejoiced in our preaching,
    when the threefold light shone from our tongue.
    But now, as when a weaned infant in the arms of a mother
    suckles on the dry breast

---

[56]The reference seems to be to the weight of Mt. Etna that Zeus cast on Typhon, the titan.

35 Χείλεσι διψαλέοισι, πόθον δ᾽ ἐψεύσατο μήτηρ,   [1388]
    Ὡς ἄρ᾽ ἐμῆς γλώσσης λαὸς ἀποκρέμαται,
    Ἰσχανόων πηγῆς πολλοῖς τὸ πάροιθε ῥεούσης,
    Ἧς νῦν οὐδ᾽ ὀλίγην ἰκμάδα οὖατ᾽ ἔχει.
    Ἄλλοι μὲν προχέουσι γλυκὺν ῥόον, οἱ δ᾽ ἀΐοντες
40 Ἄχνυντ᾽· οὐ γὰρ ἑοῦ πατρὸς ἔχουσι λόγον.
    Ποῦ μοι παννυχίων μελέων στάσις, οἷς ὑπερείδων
    Τοὺς πόδας βεβαὼς, ἔμπνοος ὥστε λίθος.
    Ἤ μοῦνος Χριστῷ ξυνούμενος, ἢ σὺν ὁμίλῳ,
    Τέρψιν ἔχων ἱερῶν ἀντιθέτων μελέων;
45 Ποῦ καμπτῶν γονάτων γλυκερὸς πόνος, ὃν προπάροιθε
    Δάκρυα θερμὰ χέον, νοῦν σκοτίην συνάγων;
    Ποῦ δὲ πενητοκόμοι παλάμαι, περὶ νοῦσον ἔπουσαι;
    Ποῦ τῆξις μελέων οἴχεται ἀδρανέων;
    Οὐκέτι μὲν θυέεσσιν ἁγνοῖς ἐπὶ χεῖρας ἀείρω,   [1389]
50 Τοῖς μεγάλοις Χριστοῦ μιγνύμενος πάθεσιν.
    Οὐκέτι δ᾽ ἀθλοφόροισι φίλην ἵστημι χορείην,
    Εὐφήμοισι λόγοις τίμιον αἷμα σέβων.
    Εὐρὼς δ᾽ ἀμφὶ βίβλοισιν ἐμαῖς, μῦθοι δ᾽ ἀτέλεστοι,
    Οἷς τίς ἀνὴρ δώσει τέρμα, φίλα φρονέων;
55 Πάντ᾽ ἔθανε ζώοντι· βίος δέ μοί ἐστιν ἀφαυρὸς,
    Νηὸς ἀκιδνότερος, τὴν λίπον ἁρμονίαι·
    Ἀλλ᾽ ἔμπης εἰ καί με, βαρύστονε δαῖμον, ἐλαύνεις,
    Οὔ ποτέ σοι κάμψω γούνατ᾽ ἐμῆς κραδίης·
    Ἀλλ᾽ ἄτρωτος, ἄκαμπτος, ἐμὴν ἐς μητέρα γαῖαν
60 Δύσομ᾽· ἔχοι σκώληξ τὴν ὄφεως δαπάνην.
    Τύπτε δορὴν, ψυχὴ δ᾽ ἄρ᾽ ἀνούτατος· εἰκόνα θείην
    Παρστήσω Χριστῷ, τὴν λάχον, ἀνδροφόνε.
    Καὶ γὰρ πρόσθε πέδησας Ἰὼβ μέγαν, ἀλλ᾽ ἐδαμάσθης,   [1390]
    Ὡς μιν ἀεθλοθέτης ἐστεφάνωσε μέγας,

35 with parched lips, and the mother deceives his hunger,
    thus the people still hang from my tongue,
    longing to encounter the stream that flowed for many
    of which now their ears cannot get even a little drop.
    True, there are others pouring forth a sweet stream, but those
        who listen
40 weep; for they do not have the word of their father.
    Where is this all-night setting of songs, relying on which
    I stand firmly on my feet, like a living rock,
    either being alone with Christ, or in community,
    when I take pleasure in antiphonal holy songs?
45 Where is the sweeter toil of bent knees, when once
    I pour out in warm tears, organizing my shadowy mind?
    Where then my hands that minister to the poor and embrace
        the sick?
    Where does the wasting away of my lifeless limbs go?
    No longer do I lift up my hands with holy offerings,
50 mixed together with the great sufferings of Christ.
    No longer do I stand in the joyful company of the victorious,
    venerating the honored blood with words of praise.
    Mold infects my books, my speeches are incomplete;
    what man will finish them, thinking kindly of them?
55 All things have died for me while I live. My life is paltry,
    shakier than a ship whose joints have failed.
    But though you still pursue me, dire devil,
    I will never bend the knees of my heart to you.
    But invincible and unconquered I will descend into
60 my mother earth. The worm instead will have the serpent's
        feast.
    Cast off the flesh, yet the soul is unharmed. To Christ I will
        present
    the divine image that I received, O murderous one.
    Even if you once bound great Job, you were subdued
    when the great judge crowned him.

65　Καὶ θῆκεν περίβωτον ἑῷ κηρύγματι νίκην,
　　Πάντα δ᾽ ἔδωκεν ἔχειν διπλᾶ, τά οἱ κέδασας.
　　Τοῖος ἐνηείης Χριστοῦ νόμος· ἀλλά μ᾽ ἄνωχθι
　　Ὀψέ περ ἀρτεμέειν· σὸς λόγος ἐστὶν ἄκος.
　　Λάζαρος ἐν νεκύεσσιν ἐγὼ νέος, ἀλλὰ βόησον,
70　Ἔγρεο, καὶ ζήτω σοῖσι λόγοισι νέκυς.
　　Λυσιμελὴς νέος εἰμὶ ὁ λέκτριος, ἀλλὰ βόησον,
　　Πήγνυσο, καὶ κλίνην βήσομαι ὕψι φέρων.
　　Σῶν κλέπτω θυσάνων παλάμαις ἄκος, ἀλλὰ ῥέεθρον
　　Αἵματος ἴσχε τάχος σαρξὶ μαραινομέναις.
75　Σοὶ δ᾽ ὑποκάμπτομ᾽ ἔγωγε, τεὸν λάχος, ὡς Χαναναία,
　　Γυρὸν ἔχουσα δέμας, ἀλλ᾽ ἀνάειρέ μ᾽, Ἄναξ.
　　Πόντος ἄνω, σοὶ δ᾽ ὕπνος ἔπι γλυκύς· ἀλλὰ τάχιστα　　[1391]
　　Ἔγρεο, καὶ στήτω σοῖσι λόγοισι σάλος.
　　Ἔστι μὲν ἄλγος ἔμοιγε, καὶ ἄψεα νοῦσος ἔχουσα.
80　Οὐ γὰρ δὴ βροτέων πάμπαν ἀμοιρέομεν,
　　Οὔτ᾽ ἐγώ, οὔτε τις ἄλλος, ἐπεὶ Θεὸς ὧδε κελεύει,
　　Μή τιν᾽ ὕπερθε φέρειν ὀφρὺν ἐπουρανίου,
　　Πάντας δ᾽ ἐς μεγάλοιο Θεοῦ λεύσσοντας ἀρωγὴν,
　　Χρειοῖ κέντρον ἔχειν πλεῖον ἐπ᾽ εὐσεβίῃ.
85　Ἀλλ᾽ ἔμπης οὐ τόσσον ὀδύρομαι εἵνεκα νούσου,
　　(Νοῦσος γὰρ νοερῷ καί τινα ῥύψιν ἔχει,
　　Ἧς πάντες χατέουσι, καὶ ὃς μάλα καρτερός ἐστι·
　　Δεσμὸς γὰρ θνητοῖς καί τι μέλαν φορέει·)
　　Ὀσσάτιον χθαμαλῶν περικήδομαι, ἄλγεα πάσχων,
90　Μή τις ὀλισθήσῃ πήμασιν ἡμετέροις.
　　Παῦροι μὲν μερόπων κρατερόφρονες, οἵ ῥα Θεοῖο　　[1392]
　　Δέχνυντ᾽ ἀσπασίως πᾶσαν ἐπιστασίην,
　　Τερπνῶν τε λυπρῶν τε, λόγον δ᾽ ἐπὶ πᾶσιν ἴσασιν,
　　Εἰ καὶ κρυπτὸν ἑῆς βένθος ἔχει σοφίης.
95　Πολλοὶ δ᾽ εὐσεβέεσσιν ἐπιθρώσκουσιν ἀκιδνοῖς.
　　Ὡς θεολατρείης οὐδὲν ἔχουσι γέρας·

65 And he rendered a celebrated victory to his proclamation,
and he gave Job double everything that you had scattered.
For such is the law of Christ's gentleness. But may Christ
bid me to rest since it is late. For your word is remedy.
I am a new Lazarus among the dead, but, come, cry out,

70 *Rise*, and let the dead man live by your words.
I am a new paralytic lying in bed, but cry out,
Be firm, and I will rise, lifting up my litter.
I snatch healing from your fringes with my hands, but stop the
    flow
of blood quickly in withering flesh.

75 I struggle for you, I am your possession, like the Canaanite
    woman,
though my body is crooked; lift me up, my king.
The sea rises, but sweet sleep is upon you. But rise up
right now, and settle the storm by your words.
This is my pain, and sickness seizes my limbs.

80 For we have no share at all in human things,
neither I, nor anyone else, since God so commands
that we not lift up some glance heavenward,
but rather that we all beg for help from the great God,
and so our neediness becomes a greater spur to piety.

85 But still I do not mourn so much because of sickness
(for sickness gives cleansing to the spiritual one,
which everyone needs, even the one who is especially strong;
for their chains also bring some darkness to mortals).
But I worry rather that as I suffer

90 someone lowly might fall because of my calamities.
Among mortals, there are few right-minded, who accept
gladly all God's governance.
In everything they know the reason for both joys and pains,
even if He should reserve some hidden depth of His wisdom.

95 But many trample on the devout when they are weak,
implying that they have no reward for their divine service.

Ἢ καὶ πάμπαν ἄτιμον ἐνὶ στήθεσσι νόημα
Ἵσταντ', αὐτομάτην πᾶν τόδε πῆξιν ἔχειν,
Οὐδὲ Θεὸν μεδέοντα βροτήσια πάντα κυβερνᾶν·
100   Οὐδὲ γὰρ ἂν τοίους οἴακας ἄμμι φέρειν.
Τῶν μνῆσαι, καὶ ἄλαλκε τεῷ θεράποντι, μέγιστε,
Μηδ' ἐπὶ λωβητὸν τέρμα βάλῃς βιότου.
Σὸς λάτρις οὗτος ἔγωγε, τεοῖς δ' ἐπὶ χεῖρας ἰάλλω
Δώροις, καὶ κεφαλαῖς τῶν ὑποκλινομένων,
105   Καὶ νούσων καλέουσιν ἀρηγόνα. Ἵλαθι, Χριστέ·   [1393]
Εἰ δέ τ' ἀποκρύπτεις, δὸς σθένος ἀθλοφόρον.
Μήτε με πάμπαν ἄτιμον ἔχοις, Λόγε, μηδ' ἐπίμοχθον,
Μήτ' ἀχάλινον ἄγοις, μήτε δυηπαθέα.
Κέντρῳ νύσσε, Μάκαρ, μὴ δούρατι· μήτε με κούφην,
110   Μηδ' ὑπεραχθομένην νῆα θάλασσα φέροι.
Καὶ κόρος ὑβρίζει, καὶ ἄλγεα νυκτὶ καλύπτει.
Ἀντιταλαντεύοις τίσιν ἀπημοσύνῃ.
Ἔσχες ἀγηνορέοντά μ', ὑπερμογέοντ' ἐλέαιρε,
Ὡς ἔτ' ἐνηείης καιρὸς, ἀριστόδικε.
115   Ἄζομ' ἐμὴν πολιήν τε καὶ ἄψεα αὐτοδάϊκτα,
Καὶ θυσίας, μογέων πήμασι, καὶ θεόθεν.
Ἀλλὰ τί μοι τὰ περισσὰ νόμους θεότητι τίθεσθαι,
Τῇ με, Χριστέ, φέροις σὸν λάτριν, ὡς ἐθέλοις.

Or else they set this utterly unworthy thought in
their hearts: that everything has its order by chance,
and God the ruler does not govern all mortal affairs:
100 nor could we handle such a helm.
Remember these things, O great one, and come to the help of
your servant,
and may you not send a grim end on my life.
For I am such a servant of yours that I place my hand on your
gifts and on the heads of those who incline to me.
105 And they call me the healer of sicknesses. Have mercy O
Christ,
and if you have hidden yourself away, give me strength for help
in battle.
And may you not leave me totally dishonored, O Logos, or
deeply burdened,
nor may you lead me rudderless or deeply suffering.
Prick me with a sting, Blessed One, and not with a spear. For
the sea cannot bear
110 my ship if it is too light or too burdened.
And satiety is arrogant, and pains lurk in the night.
May you counterbalance your punishment with protection.
You possessed me when I was valiant, take pity on me when I
am overburdened,
when there is still time for gentleness, O just judge.
115 I marvel at my old age and my crippled limbs,
and the sacrifices as I suffer in my heaven-sent pains.
But that is something extraordinary, that I make laws for the
divinity.
Christ, may you bear me your servant as you wish.

II.1.51. Θρηνητικὸν ὑπὲρ τῆς αὐτοῦ ψυχῆς.
(PG 37.1394–1396)

Πολλάκις ἱμερόεντα νέη θαλάμοισι προθεῖσα
Εἰσέτι παρθενικοῖσι νέκυν πόσιν, αἰδομένη περ,
Ἀρτίγαμος, στίλβουσα, πικρὴν ἀνεβάλλετ᾽ ἀοιδὴν,
Αἱ δέ νύ οἱ δμωαὶ καὶ ὁμήλικες ἔνθα καὶ ἔνθα
5   Ἱστάμεναι γοάουσιν ἀμοιβαδὶς, ἄλκαρ ἀνίης.
Καὶ μήτηρ φίλον υἷα νεόχνοον, οὐκέτ᾽ ἐόντα
Μύρετ᾽, ἐπ᾽ ὠδίνεσσι νέας ὠδῖνας ἔχουσα.
Καί τις ἑὴν πάτρην ὀλοφύρεται, ἣν διέπερσε
Θοῦρος Ἄρης· δόμον ἄλλος, ὃν ὤλεσεν οὐρανίη φλόξ.
10 Ψυχὴ, σοὶ δὲ γόος τις ἐπάξιος, ἣν κατέπεφνεν
Οὖλος ὄφις, πικρὸν δ᾽ ἐνομόρξατο εἰκόνι λοιγόν;   [1395]
Δάκρυε, δάκρυ᾽, ἀλιτρέ· τό σοι μόνον ἐστὶν ὄνειαρ.
Λείψω μὲν θαλίας τε ὁμηλικίην τ᾽ ἐρατεινήν·
Λείψω δ᾽ αὖ μύθων τε μέγα κλέος, εὐγενέος τε
15 Αἵματος, ὑψορόφους τε δόμους, καὶ ὄλβον ἅπαντα·
Λείψω δ᾽ ἠελίου γλυκερὸν φάος, οὐρανὸν αὐτὸν,
Τείρεα παμφανόωντα, τά τε χθὼν ἐστεφάνωται·
Ταῦτα μὲν ἐψομένοισιν. Ἐγὼ δ᾽ ὑπένερθε καρήνου
Δεσμὰ φέρων, νεκρός τε καὶ ἄπνοος, ἐν λεχέεσσι
20 Κείσομαι, ὑστατίοισι γόοις γοάοντας ἰαίνων,
Αἶνον ἔχων καὶ φίλτρον ἀδήριτον, οὐκ ἐπὶ δηρόν.
Αὐτὰρ ἔπειτα λίθος τε καὶ ἄμβροτος ἔνδοθι λώβη·
Ἀλλὰ καὶ ὣς τούτων μὲν ἐμὸν κέαρ οὐκ ἀλεγίζει,
Μούνην δὲ τρομέω καθαρὴν πλάστιγγα Θεοῖο.   [1396]
25 Ὢ μοι ἐγώ! τί πάθω; πῶς κεν κακότητα φύγοιμι;
Βένθεσιν, ἢ νεφέεσσι λαθὼν βίον; αἴθε γὰρ ἦεν

II.1.51. Lament for his soul
(PG 37.1394–1396)

Often a young girl laying out her lovely, dead husband,
on the still-virginal marriage bed, in her modesty,
just married and glowing, raises up a sad lament,
and her slaves and companions standing here and there
5   then cry out in turn, to give her courage in her pain.
And as a mother anoints her dear son, who had not yet shaved
and is no more, she groans with new birth pains.
And someone mourning his homeland, which fierce Ares
has devastated. Another mourns his home, which a fire from
      heaven has destroyed.
10   Soul, whom the coiled serpent has slain
when once he impressed a bitter poison in the image, what
      lament is fit for you?
Weep, weep, sinner! This is your lone relief.
Thus I shall leave off festivals and loving companionship.
Again I will leave off the great glory of orations, and noble
15   blood, and lofty homes, and all wealth.
I will leave off the sweet light of the sun, heaven itself,
and resplendent constellations that crown the earth.
These things are for those who follow. But here below,
with my temples bound in fetters, dead and lifeless, I will
20   lie in bed, cheering up mourners even with my final laments,
maintaining my praise and unyielding affection; yet not for too
      long.
Nevertheless, then I am a rock, with unceasing outrage within.
But indeed my heart does not worry about these things,
I fear only the honest scales of God.
25   Woe is me! Why do I suffer? How shall I flee wickedness?
By escaping life in the depths or in the clouds? Would that
      there

Ἀμπλακίης τις χῶρος ἐλεύθερος, ὥς τινα θηρῶν
Καὶ νούσων ἐνέπουσιν, ὅπως φυγὰς ἔνθεν ἵκωμαι!
Χέρσῳ μέν τις ἄλυξε πικρὴν ἅλα, ἀσπίδι δ' ἔγχος,
30 Καὶ κρυεροῦ νιφετοῖο δόμος σκέπας. Ἡ κακίη δὲ
Ἀμφίθετος, πολύχωρος, ἀφυκτοτάτη βασίλεια,
Ἠλίας πυρόεντι πρὸς οὐρανὸν ἤλυθε δίφρῳ·
Μωσῆς παιδοφόνου ποθ' ὑπέκφυγε δόγμα τυράννου,
Κητείων λαγόνων σκότιον μόρον ἁγνὸς Ἰωνᾶς,
35 Καὶ θῆρας Δανιήλ, παῖδες φλόγας. Αὐτὰρ ἔμοιγε
Τίς λύσις κακότητος; Ἄναξ, σύ με, Χριστέ, σάωσον.

2.1.52. Θρῆνος. (PG 37.1397)

Πέπονθα δεινὰ πλεῖστα, καὶ δεινῶν πέρα,
Καὶ ταῦθ' ὑφ' ὧν ἥκιστα ᾠόμην παθεῖν.
Ἀλλ' οὐδὲν οἷόν μ' οἱ κακῶς εἰργασμένοι.
Τὰ μὲν γὰρ οἴχεθ'· ὧν δ' ἔγραψεν ἡ δίκη
Βίβλοις σιδηραῖς, οἶδα τὴν μοχθηρίαν.

2.1.53. Ἕτερος θρῆνος. (PG 37.1397)

Φίλοι, πολῖται, δυσμενεῖς, ἐχθροί, πρόμοι,
Πόλλ' οἶδα πληγείς· οἶδα, ἀλλ' οὐ φάσκετε·
Βίβλοι φέρουσι ταῦτα, οὐ λήσεσθέ με.

would be some place free from sin, as there are from beasts
and illness, as they claim, so that I might flee there!
Someone avoids the bitter sea by keeping to the land, or a spear
  with a shield,

30 and a home is a refuge from frosty snow. But evil is
encompassing and vast, an inescapable kingdom.
Elijah went in a double chariot to heaven (2 Kgs 2.11).
Moses fled the decree of the child-killing king (Ex 1.15–2.10),
Holy Jonah fled his bleak lot in the innards of the whale
  (Jon 1.17)

35 and Daniel the beasts and the young men the flames
  (Dn 3.19–30; 6.16–23; 14.30–42).
Yet what release for me is there from evil? Save me, O Christ
  my king.

II.1.52. Lament (PG 37.1397)

I have suffered many terrible things, and more than terrible,
and at the hands of those by whom I would least of all think to
  suffer.
But I have suffered nothing of the sort that my enemies will
  suffer.
For my sufferings pass; but I know that justice
has inscribed their wickedness in iron books.

2.1.53. Another Lament (PG 37.1397)

Friends, countrymen, opponents, enemies, leaders,
I have known many insults; I know it, yet you say nothing.
The books report this; you will not escape me.

2.1.54. Κατὰ τοῦ πονηροῦ. (PG 37.1397–1399)

Ἦλυθες, ὦ κακοεργέ· νοήματα σεῖο γινώσκω·
Ἦλυθες, ὄφρα φάους με φίλης τ᾽ αἰῶνος ἀμέρσῃς.   [1398]
Δύσμαχε, πῶς φάος ἦλθες, ἐὼν ζόφος; οὐκ ἀπατήσεις
Ψευδόμενος. Πῶς πικρὸν ἐμοὶ μόθον αἰὲν ἀγείρεις,
5 Ἀμφαδίην λοχόων τε; τί δ᾽ εὐσεβέεσσι μεγαίρεις,
Ἐξέτι τοῦ ὅτε πρῶτον Ἀδὰμ βάλες ἐκ παραδείσου,
Πλάσμα Θεοῦ, κακίῃ δὲ σοφὴν ἐλόχησας ἐφετμήν,
Καὶ πικρὴν γλυκερῇ ζωῇ πόρσυνας ἐδωδήν;
Πῶς σε φύγω; τί δὲ μῆχος ἐμοῖς παθέεσσιν ἐφεύρω;
10 Τυτθαῖς μὲν πρώτιστον ἁμαρτάσιν, οἷα ῥέεθρον,
Ἐμπίπτεις κραδίῃσιν· ἔπειτα δὲ χῶρον ἀνοίγεις
Εὐρύτερον· μετέπειτα ῥόος θολερός τε μέγας τε
Ἦλυθες, ἄχρι χάος με λάβοι τεὸν, ἠδὲ βέρεθρον.
Ἀλλ᾽ ἀποχάζεο τῆλε, τεὰς δ᾽ ἐπὶ χεῖρας ἰάλλοις
15 Ἔθνεσιν ἢ πτολίεσσιν, ὅσαι Θεὸν οὐκ ἐνόησαν.   [1399]
Αὐτὰρ ἐγὼ Χριστοῖο λάχος, νηός τε τέτυγμαι,
Καὶ θύος· αὐτὰρ ἔπειτα θεός, θεότητι μιγείσης
Ψυχῆς. Ἀλλ᾽ ὑπόεικε Θεῷ, καὶ πλάσματι θείῳ,
Ἀζόμενος μῆνίν τε Θεοῦ, ψυχῶν τε χορείην
20 Εὐσεβέων, ἠχόν τε διηνεκέεσσιν ἐν ὕμνοις.

II.1.54. Against the enemy (PG 37.1397–1399)

You have come, O evildoer. I know your thoughts.
You have come to deprive me of the light and of my beloved
    life.
How is it, O difficult one, that but a shadow you have come as
    light? By lying
you will not trick me. How is it that you always raise painful
    battle against me,
5   both in public and through deceit? Why do you assault the
    pious,
from the very moment when you first cast Adam, God's
    creation,
out of Paradise, you assailed the wise command through your
    wickedness,
and you offered him bitter fruit in exchange for sweet life?
How shall I flee you? What shall I find as a help for my ills?
10   For you fall into hearts by means of little sins first,
like a stream. But then you open up an even
wider berth. And afterwards you come as a great and muddy
river, until chaos, now a chasm, overtakes me.
But stay back, and may you lay your hands
15   on nations or cities that do not know God.
But now I am Christ's portion, and I have become both temple
and victim; and yet then I shall be God as well, with my soul
    mixed
in divinity. But submit to God, and to God's creation;
fear the wrath of God, and the chorus of pious
20   souls, and the tune that lives in endless hymns.

II.1.55. Ἀποτροπὴ τοῦ πονηροῦ, καὶ τοῦ Χριστοῦ ἐπίκλησις.
(PG 37.1399–1401)

Φεῦγ᾽ ἀπ᾽ ἐμῆς κραδίης, δολομήχανε, φεῦγε τάχιστα·
Φεῦγ᾽ ἀπ᾽ ἐμῶν μελέων, φεῦγ᾽ ἀπ᾽ ἐμοῦ βιότου.
Κλὼψ, ὄφι, πῦρ, Βελίη, κακίη, μόρε, χάσμα, δράκων, θὴρ,
Νὺξ, λοχέ, λύσσα, χάος, βάσκανε, ἀνδροφόνε·
5   Ὅς καὶ πρωτογόνοισιν ἐμοῖς ἐπὶ λοιγὸν ἔηκας,
Γεύσας τῆς κακίης, οὔλιε, καὶ θανάτου.   [1400]
Χριστὸς ἄναξ κέλεταί σε φυγεῖν ἐς λαῖτμα θαλάσσης,
Ἠὲ κατὰ σκοπέλων, ἠὲ συῶν ἀγέλην,
Ὡς λεγεῶνα πάροιθεν ἀτάσθαλον. Ἀλλ᾽ ὑπόεικε,
10   Μή σε βάλω σταυρῷ, τῷ πᾶν ὑποτρομέει.
Σταυρὸν ἐμοῖς μελέεσσι φέρω, σταυρὸν δὲ πορείῃ,
Σταυρὸν δὲ κραδίῃ· σταυρὸς ἐμοὶ τὸ κλέος.
Οὐ λήξεις λοχόων με, κακόσχολε; οὐκ ἐπὶ κρημνοὺς,
Οὐ Σόδομα βλέψεις, οὐκ ἀθέων ἀγέλας,
15   Οἳ μεγάλην θεότητα διατμήξαντες ἔλυσαν,
Ἀλλ᾽ ἐπ᾽ ἐμὴν πολιήν, ἀλλ᾽ ἐπ᾽ ἐμὴν κραδίην;
Αἰεί με δνοφεροῖσι νοήμασιν, ἐχθρὲ, μελαίνεις,
Οὔτε Θεὸν τρομέων, οὔτε θυηπολίας.
Οὗτος καὶ Τριάδος νόος ἔπλετο ἠχέτα κήρυξ·
20   Καὶ νῦν τέρμα βλέπει. Βόρβορε, μή με θόλου,
Ὡς καθαρὸς καθαροῖσι συναντήσω φαέεσσιν   [1401]
Οὐρανίοις. Αἴγλαι, δεῦτ᾽ ἐπ᾽ ἐμὴν βιοτήν·
Τὰς δὲ χέρας τανύω, δέξασθέ με. Χαῖρε σὺ, κόσμε·
Χαῖρε, μογηροφόρε· φείδεο τῶν μετ᾽ ἐμέ.

II.1.55. Repelling the devil, and invocation of Christ
(PG 37.1399–1401)[57]

Be gone from my heart, Deceiver, be gone right now;
be gone from my limbs, be gone from my life.
Thief, snake, fire, Baal, evil, wickedness, death, chasm, dragon,
    beast,
night, assailant, madness, chaos, deceiver, murderer,
5   who even set ruin upon my forefathers,
you calamity, when you made them taste evil and death.
Christ the Lord orders you to flee into the depth of the sea,
over the cliffs, or to a herd of swine,
like that detestable Legion long ago (Mk 5.9). But submit,
10   lest I strike you with the cross, before which everything
    trembles.
I carry a cross in my limbs, a cross on my journey,
a cross in my heart. The cross is my glory.
Will you not cease assailing me, you waste of time? Will you
    not look upon the cliffs,
or Sodom, or the hordes of the godless,
15   who have destroyed the great divinity by cutting it apart,[58]
but rather upon my white hair and my heart?
You always darken me, enemy, with dusky thoughts,
fearing neither God, nor the sacrifices.
And this mind has even become the musical herald of the
    Trinity,
20   and it sees its end is now. Filthy one, do not disturb me,
so that, purified, I might meet the pure, heavenly
lights. O radiance, come to my life.
I lift my hands to you, receive me. Farewell to you, O world.
Farewell, source of anxiety. Spare those who follow me.

[57]The first nine lines of this poem appear in an amulet from the cathedral of Monza (see Simelidis, *Selected Poems*, 63). It has been dated to the second half of the sixth century, which would make this apotropaic use the oldest witness of Gregory's poems.

[58]I.e., through heretical teachings on the Trinity.

II.1.61. Θρῆνος. (PG 37.1404–1405)

Εἰκὼν κενοῦται, τίς βοηθήσει λόγος;
Εἰκὼν κενοῦται, δῶρον ἀχράντου Θεοῦ.
Ὑβρίζετ' εἰκών· αἴθομ', ὦ φθόνε, φθόνε,
Ἀλλοτρίοις λόγοις τε καὶ σοφίσμασι.
5   Πηγὴ κακῶν, μὴ βλύζε, μὴ ματαία φρήν.   [1405]
Εἰ δ' οὖν σὺ, γλῶσσα, μὴ δέχου τὸν βόρβορον.
Εἰ δ' οὖν σὺ, χείρ γε, μὴ δέχου τὰ χείρονα.
Οὕτως ἂν εἰκὼν ἡμῖν ἄφθαρτος μένη.

II.1.62. Ἱκετήρια εἰς Χριστόν. (PG 37.1405)

Μή σου λαθοίμην, μηδέ μου λάθῃς, Ἄναξ,
Ἄναξ σοφῶν μέλημα, καὶ τρισσὸν φάος·
Μή που λάθῃ με δυσμενὴς συναρπάσας,
Κευθμῶν' ἐς ἅδου, καὶ σκότου πικρὰς πύλας.
5   Δεινὸς γάρ ἐστι, καὶ λοχῶν τούς σοι φίλους
Ὅν, οἶδα, φεύξομ', εἰ σύ μου μνήμην ἔχεις,
Πυκνῶν ἀεὶ λόγοις τε καὶ νοήμασιν.

II.1.63. Θρῆνος πρὸς τὸν Χριστόν. (PG 37.1406)

Οἴμοι προσῆλθε, Χριστέ μου, πάλιν δράκων.
Οἴμοι προσῆλθε δειλιῶντί μοι σφόδρα.
Οἴμοι γέγευμαι τοῦ ξύλου τῆς γνώσεως.
Οἴμοι φθονεῖσθαι δ' ὁ φθόνος πέπεικέ με.
5   Οὔτ' εἰμὶ θεῖος, καὶ βέβλημ' ἔξω τρυφῆς.
Ῥομφαία, μικρὸν τὴν κακὴν σβέσον φλόγα,
Ὡς ἂν πάλιν δέξῃ με τῶν φυτῶν ἔσω
Χριστῷ συνεισελθόντα λῃστὴν ἐκ ξύλου.

II.1.61. Lament (PG 37.1404–1405)

The image has been erased, what word will help me?
The image has been erased, the gift of the unpolluted God.
The image is insulted. I burn, O jealous, jealous one,
with words and tricks that are foreign to me.
5   O foolish heart, you font of evils, do not burst forth.
And come, then, tongue, do not accept filth,
and come, then, hand, do not accept lower things.
Thus might our divine image remain uncorrupted.

II.1.62. Petitions to Christ (PG 37.1405)

Let me not forget you, Lord, nor you forget me,
Lord, the darling of the wise, and the triple light.
Lest the enemy should snatch me away while you are unaware,
into the depths of Hades, and the bitter gates of darkness.
5   He is terrible, and besieges your friends.
I know, I shall flee him, if you care for me,
ever strengthening me with words and insights.

II.1.63. Lament to Christ (PG 37.1406)

Alas, my Christ, the serpent approached me again.
Alas, he approached me as I cowered terribly.
Alas, I have tasted of the tree of knowledge.
Alas, the envious one persuaded me that I am envied.
5   I am not divine, and I've been cast out from delight.
Sword, extinguish the wicked flame just a bit,
so that you might again receive me among the fruitful trees,
like the thief who accompanied Christ from the cross.

Select Bibliography

Texts and Translations

Daley, Brian. *Gregory of Nazianzus. The Early Church Fathers.* London: Routledge, 2006.

Gilbert, Peter, trans. and intro. *On God and Man: The Theological Poetry of St. Gregory of Nazianzus.* Crestwood, NY: St. Vladimir's Seminary Press, 2001.

Migne, J.-P, ed. *Patrologiae Cursus Completus: Series Graeca.* Vol. 37. Paris: Migne, 1857.

Moreschini, Claudio ed. *Gregory of Nazianzus: Poemata Arcana.* Translated by D. A. Sykes. Oxford Theological Monographs. Oxford: Clarendon Press, 1997.

Simelidis, Christos. *Selected Poems of Gregory of Nazianzus: 1.2.17; II.1.10, 19, 32: A Critical Edition with Introduction and Commentary.* Göttingen: Vandenhoeck & Ruprecht, 2009.

White, Carolinne, trans. *Gregory of Nazianzus, Autobiographical Poems.* Cambridge Medieval Classics 6. Cambridge: Cambridge University Press, 1996.

Literature

Abrams Rebillard, Susan. "Speaking for Salvation: Gregory of Nazianzus as Poet and Priest in his Autobiographical Poems." PhD Diss. Brown University, 2003.

Beeley, Christopher, ed. *Re-Reading Gregory of Nazianzus.* Washington, DC: CUA Press, 2012.

Børtnes, Jostein, and Tomas Hägg, eds. *Gregory of Nazianzus: Images and Reflections.* Copenhagen: Museum Tusculanum Press, 2006.

Daley, Brian. "Walking through the Word of God." In *The Word Leaps the Gap: Essays on Scripture and Theology in Honor of Richard B. Hays,* edited by J. Ross Wagner, A. Katherine Grieb, and C. Kavin Rowe, 514–531. Grand Rapids, MI.: Eerdmans, 2008.

Gautier, Francis. *La Retraite et le Sacerdoce chez Grégoire de Nazianze*. Turnhout: Brepols, 2002.

Hilhorst, A., and J. den Boeft, eds. *Early Christian Poetry: A Collection of Essays*. Supplements to Vigiliae Christianae v. 22. Leiden: E.J. Brill, 1993.

Incontro di studiosi dell'antichità cristiana. *Motivi E Forme Della Poesia Cristiana Antica Tra Scrittura E Tradizione Classica: XXXVI Incontro Di Studiosi Dell'antichità Cristiana, Roma, 3–5 Maggio 2007*. Studia ephemeridis "Augustinianum" 108. Rome: Institutum patristicum Augustinianum, 2008.

McGuckin, John Anthony. *St. Gregory of Nazianzus: An Intellectual Biography*. Crestwood, NY: St Vladimir's Seminary Press, 2001.

Otis, Brooks. "The Throne and the Mountain." *Classical Journal* 56 (1961): 146–165.

Palla, Roberto. "Ordinamento e polimetria delle poesie bibliche di Gregorio Nazianzeno." *Wiener Studien* 102 (1989): 169–185.

Sicherl, Martin. *Die Handschriftliche Überlieferung der Gedichte Gregors von Nazianz*: 3. Die epischen und elegischen Gruppen. Studien zur Geschichte und Kultur des Altertums. Paderborn: Ferdinand Schöningh, 2011.

Sykes, Donald. "The Bible and Greek Classics in Gregory Nazianzen's Verse." In *Studia Patristica* 17.3. Edited by Elizabeth A. Livingstone, 1127–1130. Oxford: Pergamon Press, 1982.

————. "Gregory Nazianzen as didactic poet." In *Studia Patristica* 16.2, 433–437. Berlin: Peeters, 1985.

Trisoglio, Francesco. *Gregorio di Nazianzo il teologo*. Studia patristica Mediolanensia 20. Milan: Vita e pensiero, 1996.

1 *On the Priesthood* – St John Chrysostom

2 *Sermons from the Life of Saint John Chrysostom*

6 *On the Holy Icons* – St Theodore the Studite

7 *On Marriage and Family Life* – St John Chrysostom

8 *On the Divine Liturgy* – St Germanus

9 *On Wealth and Poverty* – St John Chrysostom

10 *Hymns on Paradise* – St Ephrem the Syrian

11 *On Ascetical Life* – St Isaac of Nineveh

12 *On the Soul and Resurrection* – St Gregory of Nyssa

13 *On the Unity of Christ* – St Cyril of Alexandria

14 *On the Mystical Life*, vol. 1 – St Symeon the New Theologian

15 *On the Mystical Life*, vol. 2 – St Symeon the New Theologian

16 *On the Mystical Life*, vol. 3 – St Symeon the New Theologian

17 *On the Apostolic Preaching* – St Irenaeus

18 *On the Dormition* – Early Patristic Homilies

19 *On the Mother of God* – Jacob of Serug

21 *On God and Man* – Theological Poetry of St Gregory of Nazianzus

23 *On God and Christ* – St Gregory of Nazianzus

24 *Three Treatises on the Divine Images* – St John of Damascus

25 *On the Cosmic Mystery of Christ* – St Maximus the Confessor

26 *Letters from the Desert* – Barsanuphius and John

27 *Four Desert Fathers* – Coptic Texts

28 *Saint Macarius the Spiritbearer* – Coptic Texts

29 *On the Lord's Prayer* – Tertullian, Cyprian, Origen

30 *On the Human Condition* – St Basil the Great

31 *The Cult of the Saints* – St John Chrysostom

32 *On the Church: Select Treatises* – St Cyprian of Carthage

33 *On the Church: Select Letters* – St Cyprian of Carthage

34 *The Book of Pastoral Rule* – St Gregory the Great

35 *Wider than Heaven* – Homilies on the Mother of God

36 *Festal Orations* – St Gregory of Nazianzus

37 *Counsels on the Spiritual Life* – Mark the Monk

38 *On Social Justice* – St Basil the Great

39 *The Harp of Glory* – An African Akathist

40 *Divine Eros* – St Symeon the New Theologian

41 *On the Two Ways* – Foundational Texts in the Tradition

42 *On the Holy Spirit* – St Basil the Great

43 *Works on the Spirit* – Athanasius and Didymus

44 *On the Incarnation* – St Athanasius

45 *Treasure-House of Mysteries* – Poetry in the Syriac Tradition

46 *Poems on Scripture* – St Gregory of Nazianzus

47 *On Christian Doctrine and Practice* – St Basil the Great

48 *Light on the Mountain* – Homilies on the Transfiguration

49 *The Letters* – St Ignatius of Antioch

50 *On Fasting and Feasts* – St Basil the Great

51 *On Christian Ethics* – St Basil the Great

52 *Give Me a Word* – The Desert Fathers

53 *Two Hundred Chapters on Theology* – St Maximus the Confessor

54 *On the Apostolic Tradition* – Hippolytus

55 *On Pascha* – Melito of Sardis

56 *Letters to Olympia* – St John Chrysostom

57 *Lectures on the Christian Sacraments* – St Cyril of Jerusalem

58 *The Testament of the Lord*

59 *On the Ecclesiastical Mystagogy* – St Maximus the Confessor

60 *Catechetical Discourse* – St Gregory of Nyssa

61 *Hymns of Repentance* – St Romanos the Melodist

62 *On the Orthodox Faith* – St John of Damascus

63 *Headings on Spiritual Knowledge* – Isaac of Nineveh

64 *On Death and Eternal Life* – St Gregory of Nyssa

65 *The Prayers of Saint Sarapion* – Saint Sarapion of Thmuis

ST VLADIMIR'S SEMINARY PRESS
1-800-204-2665 • www.svspress.com

We hope this book has been enjoyable and edifying for your spiritual journey toward our Lord and Savior Jesus Christ.

One hundred percent of the net proceeds of all SVS Press sales directly support the mission of St Vladimir's Orthodox Theological Seminary to train priests, lay leaders, and scholars to be active apologists of the Orthodox Christian Faith. However, the proceeds only partially cover the operational costs of St Vladimir's Seminary. To meet our annual budget, we rely on the generosity of donors who are passionate about providing theological education and spiritual formation to the next generation of ordained and lay servant leaders in the Orthodox Church.

Donations are tax-deductible and can be made at www.svots.edu/donate. We greatly appreciate your generosity.

To engage more with St Vladimir's Orthodox Theological Seminary, please visit:

www.svots.edu
online.svots.edu
www.svspress.com
www.instituteofsacredarts.com